# ALBERTO

# GIACOMETTI

1. THE STUDIO
1949 - Oil on canvas, 63 × 93 cm
Tate Gallery, London

# Alberto Giacometti

BY

BERNARD LAMARCHE—VADEL

Translated by

Kit Currie

THE WELLFLEET PRESS
WELLFLEET

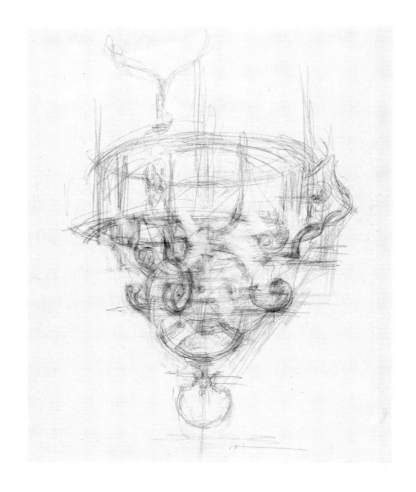

2. THE CHANDELIER AT STAMPA
   1963 - Pencil drawing, 50 × 32.5 cm
   Private collection

Published by
WELLFLEET PRESS
110 Enterprise Avenue
Secaucus, New Jersey 07094

Copyright © 1984 Nouvelles Éditions Françaises, Paris

English translation copyright © 1989 William S. Konecky Associates

ISBN: 1-55521-474-6

Printed and bound in Hong Kong

3. STUDIO: DOG, CAT, PICTURE
ca. 1935 - Lithograph
Private collection

# Preface

The work of Alberto Giacometti, sculptor, painter, and draftsman, has strong literary connections, as does that of some other great artists of the twentieth century—Balthus, Bacon, and Bram van Velde.

While Giacometti always affirmed that he was preoccupied with problems of perception and optics, his work was refined very early on by psychological, philosophical, moral, and emotional commentary. Numerous poets and writers such as Jean Genet, Michel Leiris, and Jean-Paul Sartre have contributed toward an appreciation of Giacometti's work.

The question remains, however, of why a real effort at comprehending the work's plastic dimension has only recently been attempted, in contrast to the extraordinary fame that Giacometti's name enjoys, which Picasso acknowledged as the only one equal to his own.

Undoubtedly we must take into account the power of the myth that the artist's life already represents. The last of the great artists of Montparnasse, a habitué of cafés, a night reveler, continuing to live in the same wretched studio and follow the same way of life when celebrity and its consequent ease

overtook him, Giacometti embodied all the attributes of the image that society saw as representative of the romantic dream of genius and misfortune.

Much of the gossip about Giacometti has held a fascination for writers, and later, the public, as it portrays him as prey to the grief of not being able to complete an undertaking except by constantly endeavoring to perform the impossible. This image is recorded in the work of James Lord, who describes sitting for his portrait by Giacometti, drawing us into the intimacy of the artist's life and ideas. Lord has given us the best introduction to this art of powerlessness through which the artist has unceasingly decried exigency and fate.

It is true that the iconography of Giacometti's face is an endless catalogue of the unfolding of anxiety and care, of grief and of the stamp of age upon character (ills. 4, 255, 256). The great photographers Brassaï, Man Ray, Cartier-Bresson, and Scheidegger, among others, were never deceived about this. They caught his features and illuminated his sensibility, often relating the features and bearing to representations of the work.

Giacometti is surely the least recognized of the great artists, and we must begin the difficult task of evaluating the importance of his contribution to the field of modern sculpture. We must stand back a little from the obstructing literary or poetic commentary, which has always hindered a direct approach to those difficult works of Giacometti that are set midway between statuary art and sculpture.

Now we should ask ourselves if the importance and the sometimes excellence of this commentary is not the organic result of the artist's very technique, which would perhaps signify that this work itself is the result of a combination of ideas that prevailed in its construction. We cannot disregard the conformity of Giacometti's ideas with two major currents of thought in his time: Surrealism and then existentialism. Given this point of view, clearly, the interest shown by André Breton and the friendship of Sartre and his circle reveal an identity of views with two successive periods of the artist's activity, which is confirmed by Simone de Beauvoir in her memoirs.[1]

It would then be justifiable to ask ourselves what is the hidden content of these works, for their author's life so often furnished a moral model that his friendships and intellectual interests must have had a significant bearing on his work.

During the second half of his life, the wish—constantly attested to by his visitors—"to be able to make a head, one head, just once," and the repeated feeling of obstruction and having to start again, made Giacometti the embodiment of the archetypical exigency of the modern artist since Cézanne, faced by what he sees or in terms of what he conceives. To penetrate experiences to establish principles is the fate of the modern artist, each in his own way; and in the production of the figure, he reflects the conditions of that production. That is surely the abstraction of modern art.

Stubbornly remodeling, erasing, overpainting, effacing, lengthening, subtracting, and retrieving in search of the truth of one head, one head once, Giacometti first busied himself in offering us a figure that represents the deception of the visible, its uncertain and impossible character, making possible a drawing of distance and crossing the distance between the head one sees and the head conceived by distance, which approaches a depiction of the invisible.

However we perceive the legend of the last of the great bohemians of the Paris school, it is his work's own meaning that must occupy us, the clue to the urgency that first led Giacometti to recognize the language of his time and the importance of the stylistic base that Cubism represented for his generation.

Undoubtedly Surrealism was for the artist the only means leading to an immediate expression of certain plastic experiences concerning the unformulated record of a person gripped by desires, doubts, and lacerations of the unconscious.

In 1935 Giacometti came to grips with the radical question of representing reality and, therefore, of seeing, whose answer was to be the object of a lifelong quest.

This study concerns the entire diachronic expanse of his work, which constantly interpreted its cultural substratum, in whose image it often offered the greatest understanding. If Giacometti was one of the great artists of the twentieth century, he was one who reached the heights of legibility of his time in work that itself remains an enigma of invisibility striving to conquer reality.

---

1. Simone de Beauvoir, *Laforce de l'age* (Paris: Gallimard, 1960), 556ff.

5. SELF-PORTRAIT
1918 - India ink drawing, 37 × 25 cm
Kupferstichkabinett, Kunstmuseum, Basel

6. MOUNTAIN LANDSCAPE
1916–19 - Watercolor, 13.5 × 24.3 cm
Kunstmuseum, Basel

# I – The Formative Years (1915–1922)

Few twentieth-century artists have been so attached to, and influenced by, their native country as Giacometti. While living in Paris, each year at vacation time he would take the road to Switzerland and the valley of Bregaglia in the southwest where he was born.

This area of Italian Switzerland stretches north to Saint Moritz and the Swiss Protestant culture, and south toward Milan and Como, where the Italian influence is predominant. The landscape is mostly mountainous and wooded, but also agricultural around the little village of Stampa. In 1906 the Giacometti family settled in the middle of the region in a large elegant house, which the artist's father rented from Alberto's uncle, Otto Giacometti, for a small sum. A family of artists and confectioners, the Giacomettis had been in the valley for several generations. Alberto's family was one of remarkably gifted artists. His father, Giovanni Giacometti, was a talented painter whose three sons each adopted an artistic career. Besides Alberto, Diego was to be an artist-artisan and creator of

original furniture, while Bruno would dedicate himself to architecture. In 1900 Giovanni Giacometti married Annetta Stampa, from the neighboring village of Borgonovo, where the young couple first settled down in a house belonging to the wife's family. It was here, on 10 October 1901, that Alberto Giacometti was born.

The great sculptor's childhood in the Bregaglia region, first at Borgonovo, then at Stampa, was also spent at Maloja-Capolago, where the family passed their summer holidays and Christmas and New Year's. North of Borgonovo, this village was in a wooded region at the southernmost end of Lake Sils.

Beyond the enlightened artistic education that Giovanni Giacometti gave his children, the area in which Alberto spent his childhood, the rural customs of the mountain people, the way they occupied their time, and the hardy character of the inhabitants of the valley would leave an indelible mark on the young sculptor. When Giacometti was famous, in numerous interviews, he recalled with

9

7. POTS OF FLOWERS
   1913 - Pencil drawing, 34 × 25.5 cm
   Alberto Giacometti Foundation, Zurich

8. MOUNTAIN LANDSCAPE
   1916–19 - Watercolor, 13.5 × 24.3 cm
   Alberto Giacometti Foundation, Zurich

great feeling his childhood surroundings, which were to constitute a major reference point in his art and in his life.

Resembling a prewar Italian mason, with whom he was often compared, with his rough speech and highlander's manners, Giacometti stayed faithful all his life to the rugged simplicity of the people of Stampa. And in their turn, as Franz Meyer observed, the strong individuality and solid identity of the village people forged the strong personality of Giacometti and the direct, open, and friendly relations he had with his fellow painters, poets, and writers in Paris. At the same time this strong psychological foundation gave him an endurance that yielded only to the inner necessities of his art. The urgency and constancy that marked the highest point of his life and his work, whose paradigm is the representation of man, requires an examination of his apprenticeship at Stampa to discover there the place of his first awakening to the basic idea of his work.

Furthermore, the mountainous configuration of the valley of Bregaglia, from Stampa to Maloja-Capolago, also gave form to the village that would haunt Giacometti's later spatial conceptions.

Yves Bonnefoy writes: "The mountain at Stampa is so bare that it is reduced to mere existence." Below Stampa on the massifs of the Engadine, there are forests of chestnut and larch, which Giacometti remembered vividly: "For many years of my childhood, in one corner of the forest, the straight, bare trunks (without branches almost to their tops), through which blocks of gneiss could be seen, always seemed to me like people who had stopped in midstride to speak to each other." But the form of the village where Giacometti had spent his entire youth also produced a lasting impression on his sense of space. The village of Stampa may be visualized as a passage that follows the course of the valley, where the high walls of the houses are in immediate relation to the open airiness of the central street. At the end of the block of houses, the countryside rises in a harmonious hierarchy, which leads to the peaks of two thousand meters overlooking the valley. This organic relation between near and far, where all parts of the landscape are of equal value in the arrangement of the view, certainly influenced Giacometti's very personal ideas of distance in space and its relation to scale.

From his earliest years, Alberto was in direct contact with artistic creation. As soon as the family was settled in Stampa, his father converted a barn into a studio where the young child could begin to draw. Giovanni Giacometti (1868–1934), a talented painter, involved in the newest artistic investigations of his time, was his son's first teacher. Initiated successively into Divisionism, Symbolism, Cubism, and Futurism, Giovanni Giacometti had a distinct predilection for Ferdinand Hodler and Cézanne, but he could interrupt his investigation of the birth of abstraction by the avowal that he "could get absolutely nothing out of Kandinsky."

This European cultural openness of the artist's father, however, did not lead to the assertion of a personal style; and after 1900 it was rather the whole development of Swiss art that linked father and son for a quarter of a century.

Besides Ferdinand Hodler, whose importance as a European painter was recognized in 1920, before which time he had been considered only an important representative of Swiss art, Giovanni Giacometti had ties with a distant relative in his own village, Augusto Giacometti, and also with Cuno Amiet, Alberto's godfather, both artists. In the bosom of this group of artists who represented the best of Swiss art, the young Alberto followed the impassioned debates of the protagonists of the new art forms, and undoubtedly his father had a definite influence on him, while at the same time lending unconditional support to his son's own experiments.

Until the age of eighteen, Alberto received a diversified artistic education in his father's studio, which allowed him to spend as much time copying the old masters—a habit he kept—as he spent immersing himself in the confusion of the great movements of modern art being born before his eyes and which his father embraced so fervently. The heritage of these eighteen years in Switzerland, in which Giacometti learned technique, composition, and art history, is the fundamental basis from which he rapidly developed his rich personality.

First of all, undoubtedly, we must emphasize the multiplicity of references that his father embraced and discarded before Alberto's eyes. Beyond classical painting, these references were van Gogh, Gauguin, Cézanne, Fauvism, and the Expressionism of the group known as Die Brücke, all of whose different styles the younger Giacometti could identify.

But clearly the twin influences of Cézanne and Hodler had left their stamp on Alberto's development, and much later, against the advice of the Surrealists, he did not fail to recognize his debt to the master of Aix.

The boundaries for any debate on Swiss art are delimited by two influences: the relation between its German and French elements, and the powerful national tradition. This tradition, retained by Giacometti, primarily determines the moral content of those works of art in which a human being is a major motif. The frontality of the representation,

9. LANDSCAPE WITH FIELD AND TREES
1916–19 - Watercolor, 19 × 22 cm
Alberto Giacometti Foundation, Zurich

10. TREES SEEN FROM THE STUDIO AT STAMPA
ca. 1922 - Watercolor, 31 × 21.5 cm
Alberto Giacometti Foundation, Zurich

11. TREES
    1918 - Pen drawing, 34 × 25 cm
    Mr. and Mrs. Adrien Maeght collection

12. STUDY OF A MOUNTAIN LANDSCAPE
   1916–19 · Watercolor, 23.7 × 30.9 cm
   Kunstmuseum, Basel

13. THE ARTIST'S MOTHER
1913–14 - Pencil drawing, 36.5 × 24.5 cm
Alberto Giacometti Foundation, Zurich

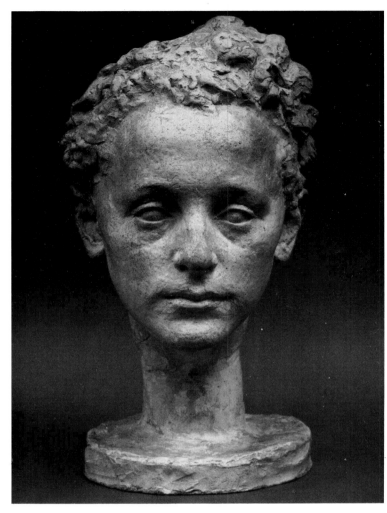

14. BUST OF BRUNO
1919 - Plaster, 39.7 × 21 × 24 cm
Alberto Giacometti Foundation, Zurich

bound to a certain formal austerity, constitutes the basis of a demand for the viewer's moral commitment. The expressiveness of Hodler's work and the constructive logic of Cézanne's now allowed Giacometti to realize drawings and paintings in which his mastery of "fibrous" contour was already affirmed, as was the rigor of construction, and a relative smoothness—the watermark of the masters.

If his father's studio furnished Alberto with great models with which to identify himself, his godfather, Cuno Amiet (1868–1961), was also able to offer him valuable information on Gauguin and the Pont-Aven school, to which Gauguin had belonged.

If Cuno Amiet's art at that time hardly exceeded a mastery of post-Impressionism, it nevertheless allowed the young artist to ponder Gauguin's theories on color and his rejection of academic naturalism. But also from Gauguin, by way of Cuno Amiet, comes the idea of style—ultimately so important in Giacometti's art—that is, the autonomous style of the primitive and Egyptian art from which Gau-

guin and then Giacometti would derive a mode of expression.

Alberto Giacometti was a very precocious artist. From the age of nine he made illustrations for fairy tales ("Snow White"), and the following year he was drawing from life. His vocation for the portrait was already established, though he showed considerable mastery of landscape and still life painting.

Giacometti's was a happy childhood in which his gifts were vigorously encouraged. In 1913 he completed his first painting, *Still Life with Apples*; then in 1914 his father gave him a block of plastiline, and Alberto made his first sculpture, a bust of his brother Diego. Having finished primary school at Stampa in 1915, he entered the Protestant college at Schiers, near Coire, where he met and formed friendships with Christophe Bernoulli and Lucas Lichtenhahn (ills. 19, 20), who would become curator at the Kunstmuseum of Basel; they would remain friends throughout his life. With his parents' permission, he obtained a small studio for his own

15. DIEGO
ca. 1920 - Pencil drawing, 49.5 × 30.5 cm
Alberto Giacometti Foundation, Zurich

16. DIEGO
1919 - Oil on canvas, 25.5 × 19 cm
Mr. and Mrs. Adrien Maeght collection

use at Schiers; here he spent his free time painting and sculpting, but also reading the German romantics Goethe and Hölderlin, as well as books on natural history and history.

After easily reproducing what he saw with a feeling of absolute sovereignty, for the first time Giacometti encountered difficulties; his models eluded him and diminished oddly. He hesitated over choosing a career as a painter, sculptor, or chemist. He asked his father for three months to consider his choice, a request that was easily granted. By the end of that time, he had decided to be an artist. At the age of eighteen, he enrolled in the Ecole des Beaux-Arts in Geneva.

The painting studio was under the direction of David Estoppey (1862–1952), a former pupil of Barthélémy Menn, the well-known Impressionist painter. Alberto soon discovered that he had made a mistake; the loneliness and the difficulties that he encountered in the realization of his artistic projects led him to break with the school. Probably we should mention here some traces of family influence; some decades before both his father, Giovanni, and his godfather, Augusto, had themselves left a school of fine arts after only eight days and had immediately entered a school of applied arts. Alberto likewise enrolled in the Ecole des Arts et Métiers in Geneva, attending a sculpture class under the direction of Maurice Sarkissof, a friend of Archipenko's.

Two years later in 1921, when Alberto had just reached twenty, his father was appointed head of the Swiss section of the Venice Biennale. He took his son to Italy; and this first journey of Alberto's was of prime importance in his education as an artist. For the first time, in Venice, the young artist was confronted by the definitive manifestation of the masterpiece. Tintoretto's vision was a revelation for him. The Venetian's dynamic light, at once monumental and theatrical, confirmed his feelings

17. GIAN-ANDREA STAMPA
   1919–20 - Pencil drawing, 29.1 × 22.1 cm
   Burckhardt-Koechlin Collection
   Kupferstichkabinett, Kunstmuseum, Basel

18. RENATO STAMPA
   1919–20 - Pencil drawing, 40 × 29 cm
   Alberto Giacometti Foundation, Zurich

19. LUCAS LICHTENHAHN
   ca. 1918 - Pencil drawing, 29.4 × 24.2 cm
   Alberto Giacometti Foundation, Zurich

20. LUCAS LICHTENHAHN
   1917–18 - Linocut, 28.5 × 21.9 cm
   Kupferstichkabinett, Kunstmuseum, Basel

21. DIEGO AND HIS DOG
    ca. 1918 - Blue ink drawing, 30 × 22.5 cm
    Private collection

22. BRUNO WITH ATLAS
1922 - Pencil drawing, 21.5 × 29 cm
Mr. and Mrs. Adrien Maeght collection

about his first attempts, but the powerful drawing also confirmed the need to copy incessantly and recognize the power of delineation. While in Venice he also copied Bellini and the mosaics at Saint Mark's. Then, he set off for Padua, toward the contradictory revelation of Giotto.

After the swirling space of Tintoretto's compositions and the exaltation of color in his cosmic vision, Giacometti discovered the Venetian's complete antithesis in Giotto. After Tintoretto's expressive, sometimes grandiloquent, theatricality, he found the inwardness, the measured gesture, the severe architecture, and the restful spiritual harmony of Giotto.

For the remainder of his life, his artistic road lay between these two contradictory reference points; and if Giacometti so often stated his adherence to the art of Cézanne, it was because he saw in it the highest attempt to reconcile the strength of expression with the necessity of structure.

The same evening of his discovery of Giotto in Padua, he had a sudden vision while watching a group of two or three young girls strolling along the streets. The girls appeared to him to become huge, a frightening violence in their movements as if some magic force had channeled a supernatural energy into this everyday reality. This shattering experience of the total enigma of reality would continue to haunt the artist; and he decided to go beyond art, to abandon his satisfaction in the mastery of reproducing the visible in order to create the plastic equivalent of the violence of reality. During this same year, the young artist made a second journey, first to Florence, where he discovered Egyptian art through a bust in the archaelogical museum: "The first head that seemed to me a likeness," he said. Then in order to deepen his knowledge of Egyptian art, Giacometti went alone to Rome to explore the Vatican collections. At this time he also discovered the importance of the baroque statuary of Bernini and Borromini. Drawn by the Byzantine mosaics there, he traveled to Naples, Pompeii, and Paestum. Between Florence and Rome, at Assisi Giacometti discovered Cimabue, who seemed to him an impressive compromise between the intensity of Giotto and the light of Tintoretto.

23. BRUNO ASLEEP
    1920 - Oil on canvas, 33 × 46 cm
    Private collection, Zurich

## The Copies

As it is impossible for me to assign precise dates to most of these copies, I will try to give a chronological summary of them. Ever since I saw reproductions of works of art, going right back to my childhood, I always wanted to copy immediately those that attracted me the most, and this pleasure in copying has never left me.

The copies shown are only a small portion of all that I have done, many are lost, especially those from originals in notebooks; suddenly I see myself in Rome at the Borghese Gallery, copying a Rubens, one of my great finds of the day, but at the same moment I see myself also going back through

24. HEAD OF A PROPHET
Pencil drawing, 27.5 × 19 cm

25. CHRIST PANTOCREATOR
Pencil drawing, 29 × 21 cm

26. THE MEDICI TOMB AT SAN LORENZO, FLORENCE
Ballpoint pen drawing, 28 × 21 cm

all my past; near the window in Stampa, about 1914, concentrating on copying a Japanese print—I could describe all the details—then Rembrandt's *The Supper*, and then a Pinturicchio rushes forward and all the frescoes of the fifteenth-century painters in the Sistine Chapel, but I can also see myself some four years later going home to my studio in Paris in the evening, turning the pages of books and copying this or that Egyptian sculpture or a Carolingian miniature, as well as a Matisse. How to explain all this? All the art of the past, of all epochs and all civilizations comes together before me, simultaneously, as if space had taken the place of time.

Alberto Giacometti
4 October 1965

27. ST. FRANCIS, AFTER CIMABUE
    Pencil drawing, 33 × 26 cm

28. LAOCOÖN, AFTER A STATUE IN THE VATICAN MUSEUM
    Ballpoint pen drawing, 29 × 21 cm

29. EGYPTIAN DRAWING
    Ballpoint pen drawing, 50 × 32 cm

21

30. GIOVANNI GIACOMETTI: PORTRAIT OF ALBERTO GIACOMETTI
1922 - Pencil drawing, 41.7 × 30 cm
Alberto Giacometti Foundation, Zurich

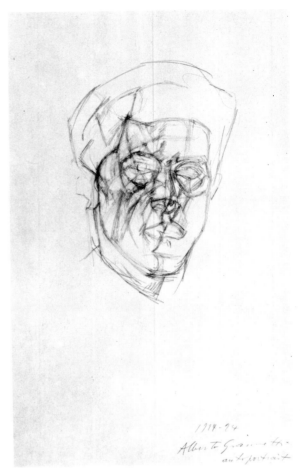

31. SELF-PORTRAIT
1922–24 - Pencil drawing, 50 × 32.5 cm
Kupferstichkabinett, Kunstmuseum, Basel

While executing these numerous copies during his stay in Rome, Giacometti painted portraits in the Pointillist style, went to the opera, to concerts, and read and illustrated the Greek tragedies. Also, in Rome he discovered Italian Futurism. Staying with an uncle, he also worked hard at two busts of his cousin Bianca, which he would destroy before leaving the city.

In summation, we may say that this sojourn in Rome, in the best tradition of a young artist desiring to perfect his art, was an experience for Alberto that allowed him to grasp the nature of the rapport between nature and art. His discovery of the great works of art confirmed him in his intuition that the object of art is not to reproduce reality, but to create an autonomous reality of the same intensity. This would remain the enigmatic object of his art.

From this period also comes a dramatic story that never ceased to haunt the sculptor's conscience. While he was traveling in the south of Italy, the young man became friends with an old Dutch librarian, whom we know only as van M.

In the autumn of 1921, through the intermediary of an announcement in the press, van M. asked Giacometti to meet him in the Tyrol. In a room in an inn, Alberto witnessed the final agonies and death of his friend. Seated at the bedside of the dying man, reading a work of Maupassant on Flaubert, Giacometti tried to draw the head of the sick man, the nose that was becoming more and more prominent, the hollow cheeks, the half-open mouth, the feeble breathing, the deep wrinkles. But he could not do it. Only in 1947, would he again experience the impossibility of capturing the totality of the body being consumed by death. With the sculpture *Head on a Rod* (ill. 178), he would approach once again that tragic and singular event that had made him conscious of death and time. His work would continue to exhibit the irresistible attraction of these two themes.

22

32. SELF-PORTRAIT
1921 - Oil on canvas, 82.5 × 72 cm
Alberto Giacometti Foundation, Zurich

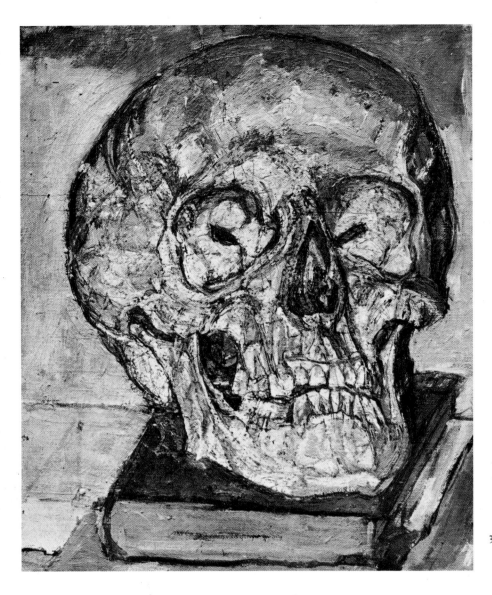

33. THE SKULL
1923 - Oil on canvas, 30 × 24 cm
Private collection, Paris

## Settling in Paris

Once more at his father's instigation, in 1922 Giacometti, who would have preferred to study in Vienna, where Hodler had acquired international renown, went alone to Paris, where between other tenancies he would occupy Archipenko's empty studio. Giacometti explained his choice: "My father thought it would be beneficial for me to work in an independent school, as he himself had done in his youth; there I would be able to draw and paint; I was at first opposed to the idea; my father didn't insist and it was this that finally made me go."

Settled in Paris on 1 January 1922, Giacometti divided his time between Antoine Bourdelle's modeling courses each morning at the Academie de la Grande Chaumière and intensive practice of draw-

ing and modeling in his hotel each afternoon. Though some months later he was to move again to Archipenko's studio, he was never his pupil; they had simply been friends since their meeting in Geneva.

This first stay in Paris, thanks to which Giacometti could perfect his studies, was a period of great loneliness for the young sculptor, as well as one of hard work and doubt. He visited all the museums, the Louvre especially, and copied the works of Egyptians, the Middle Ages, and Matisse.

In his famous letter of 1947 written to Pierre Matisse, which was to assure the wide acceptance of his work in the United States and remain the autobiographical basis for the study of his life and direc-

24

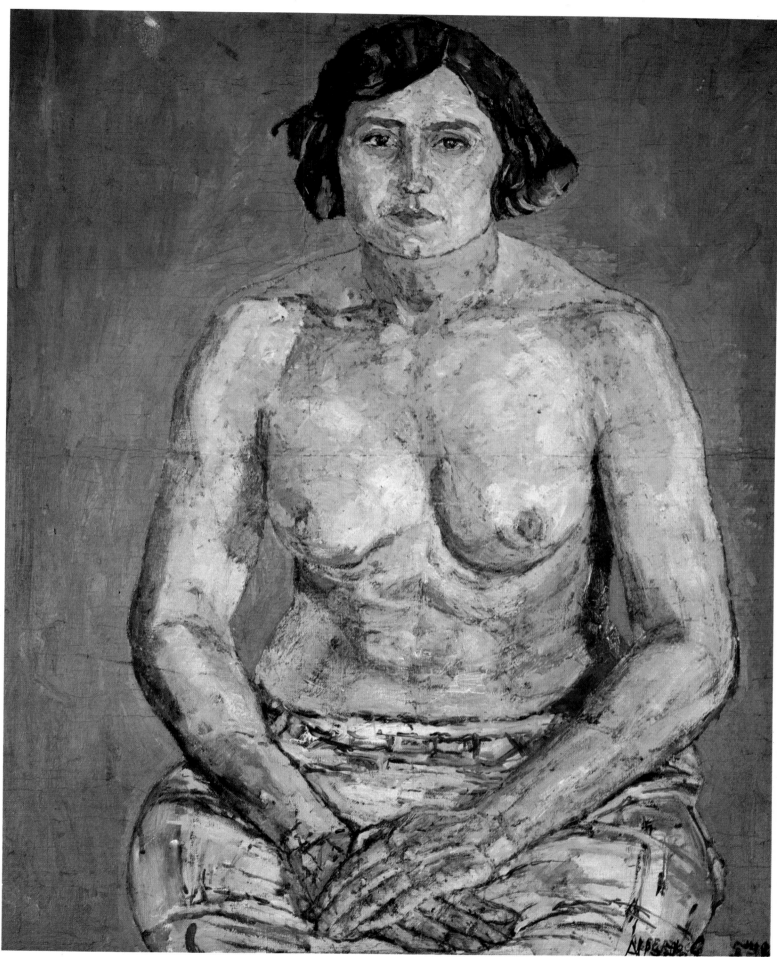

34. NUDE
    1923 - Oil on canvas, 61 × 50 cm
    Alberto Giacometti Foundation, Zurich

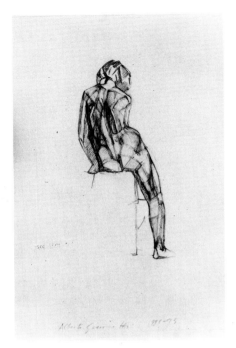

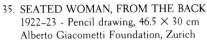

35. SEATED WOMAN, FROM THE BACK
1922–23 - Pencil drawing, 46.5 × 30 cm
Alberto Giacometti Foundation, Zurich

36. SEATED NUDE, FROM THE BACK
1922–23 - Pencil drawing, 48.5 × 31.5 cm
Alberto Giacometti Foundation, Zurich

37. STANDING NUDE WITH RAISED ARM, FROM
THE BACK
1922–23 - Pencil drawing, 41 × 26 cm
Alberto Giacometti Foundation, Zurich

tion, Giacometti underlines once more the mounting difficulties that he met with in the creation of a figure: "It seemed impossible to grasp the whole thing (we were much too close to the model, and if you began with a detail, a fingernail or a nose, there would never be any hope of getting the whole). But, if on the other hand, you started by analyzing a detail, the tip of a nose, for example, you were lost. You could spend your whole life on it and never get anywhere. The shape would come apart; it would be no more than particles drifting on a vast black emptiness, the distance between one side of a nose and the other is limitless as the Sahara, nothing is stable, everything eludes you."

More and more strongly influenced by Cézanne, Giacometti confined himself one winter to drawing only one subject: a skull (ill. 33). This is revealing of his mental disposition and of his mature technique. Giacometti never repudiated Cézanne, following his example of colliding head-on with his subject. In the presence of Mount Sainte-Victoire, Cézanne had begun the diligent approach to that feeling for color that led him to register on his easel only the fundamental principles of structure and shape. Giacometti was continuing Cézanne's work at this time, but in the reverse. When he resolved, particularly in his drawings, to outline only the essential vectors of his subject, his aim was not to simplify or release the graphic essence of a representation; it was to find the difficult path toward a total reconstruction of his subject, a totality that eluded him and whose elusive-

ness was his despair. For him also the issue of construction, that is, the localized identity of form, and feeling was not one and the same. On the contrary, for him it was the antagonism between the subject as it is and the subject as perceived in an emotive sequence of constituent glances, which remained the most powerful mystery that this young artist continually sought to solve.

Having escaped from the importunate law of the reality of the subject and the proof of its permanent flight, Giacometti began to work from memory, which allowed him to grasp the particulars of the subject in the newfound unity of form and emotional content connected to it.

In 1925 Giacometti moved into his first Paris studio at 37, rue Froidevaux; he continued to study with Bourdelle, but began to acquaint himself with the works of the preceding generation of artists— the sculptors Gonzalez, Laurens, Arp, Lipchitz; and the painters Masson, Miró, Freundlich, Duchamp, and Picasso. Through them Giacometti also became aware of the formal importance of primitive art, African and Oceanic, and of the sculpture of the Cyclades, whose vogue had lasted for twenty years in Paris.

Although the importance of Giacometti's five years with Antoine Bourdelle should not be exaggerated, it would be quite unjustified to minimize its significance, even though Giacometti later declared that the master's influence on his pupil was almost nil.

At this time, as we have seen, Giacometti was subject to a bundle of contradictory influences,

26

38. STANDING MAN, WITH CLASPED HANDS
1922–23 - Pencil drawing, 37 × 18 cm
Alberto Giacometti Foundation, Zurich

39. THREE NUDE WOMEN
1923–24 - Pencil drawing, 44.5 × 28 cm
Alberto Giacometti Foundation, Zurich

40. SEATED NUDE WOMAN
1921–22 - Pencil drawing, 44.5 × 28 cm
Alberto Giacometti Foundation, Zurich

none of which, except for that of Cézanne, exercised exclusive control over the young artist. It is true that the influence of Bourdelle or, through him, Rodin, is not really discernible. As Reinhold Hohl established, it seems that the master's influence on the pupil was more on the theoretical and moral level than on the actual. Those statements we have from Bourdelle on the preeminence of drawing and the never-ending activity of the draftsman that a sculptor must pursue are the same ones that Giacometti himself would later accept. In the same way, the supreme importance of the model of the human face and the necessity to return to it continually to understand the relationship between the whole and the parts were ideas common to both artists.

Although the relations between the two artists were undoubtedly difficult, it was Bourdelle who invited Giacometti to exhibit at the Salon des Tuileries that same year, 1925. The young sculptor showed two works, which represent the contradictory oscillations of his preoccupations at that time. The *Head of Diego* is in a traditional vein; while the sculpture *Torso* (ill. 44), if not innovative, does indicate the lively interest that the artist had in the post-Cubist avant-garde. Bourdelle said of it: "It's the sort of thing one might do at home, but one would never exhibit it." A fair judgment, but too severe since *Torso* represents the first radical break with traditional sculpture in Alberto's work, and is at the same time his first effort to synthesize those diverse influences that gave him access to the sensibility of his time.

In the differences between the two sculptures shown at the Salon des Tuileries, *Torso* and the *Head of Diego*, or even between them and the *Bust of Joseph Müller*, Giacometti's first commission in that same year, we see the fundamental tension between style and reality that remains the key to understanding the work of this master. Bourdelle was not mistaken in inviting the young sculptor: both the *Head of Diego* and the *Bust of Joseph Müller* are finished works that exploit all the resources of academic art to create a likeness to the model. They typify Giacometti's mastery of traditional techniques, which since his first crisis in 1919, the artist had put to furious test, for this mastery could not render an equivalent of the reality he perceived as fleeting and ephemeral. It was more the reality of the rules, of conventional contingencies, of the world's reality that he reproduced from his model, rather than the fragmented reality of the model in space and movement. We know that because of his own experience of perception and that of his colleagues, Giacometti well understood that he must hold fast in his pursuit of reality, must seek the irreducible elements of form, its essence, its most elusive outline. Between the restoration of the whole, and that of the separate details, in order to resolve these contradictory attempts to render reality, Giacometti would choose the plastic result of a structural composition. It was above all the choice of a style, Cubism, and it would constitute the first great period of the sculptor's work.

41. SELF-PORTRAIT
1923–24 - Pencil drawing, 27.5 × 23 cm
Alberto Giacometti Foundation, Zurich

# II – The Cubist Period (1925-1929)

With *Torso* (ill. 44), Giacometti appears to change tradition. Leaving behind the classical style of the busts of Diego and Müller, *Torso* takes its place in the youthful tradition of the avant-garde.

The Cubist period inaugurated by this piece was later replaced by the Surrealist phase, both preceding Giacometti's mature work created under the shadow of existentialist philosophy. This phase, too often mentioned in attempts to give a full account of the evolution of the sculptor's work although it helps us penetrate the artist's vision, is nonetheless quite superficial. Certainly the friendships he maintained and the influences he acknowledged enabled him to span diverse intellectual communities; and, of course, the successive stages of his work mark his successive interests. We must, however, first understand that since the first crisis of 1919, Giacometti was seeking only one object—reality. All phases of his work are simply the same transstylistic operation of appropriating reality.

By casting aside the conventional criteria for replicating a model, Giacometti pursued his quest beyond verisimilitude, perceiving at the same time its illusory character and its unique province—the mastery of surface and volume.

His unrelenting realism, like Picasso's, though both had toyed with abstract art, entailed breaking the assumptions about the essence of representative form. Although for the short period of four years he embraced the characteristics of Cubism, it was not because he believed for a moment that the Cubist doctrine of an angled combination of planes could be the answer to a definitive restatement of reality. For Giacometti, the synthetic theory of Cubism was to be only a temporary means of access to three basic elements of his subsequent work. These elements would be found fully affirmed, though modified, during his Surrealist period.

In his radical search for the totality of ways in which an object may be seen, the Cubist denies the artist's right to one particular view of the object he is reproducing, under penalty, within the limits of classical perspective, of affirming an optical illusion, instead of that object's entire reality.

In place of a single view of an object, Cubism substitutes several simultaneous views from different standpoints. Thus when the object is cut into angled planes, the eye sees the obverse, the reverse, and the side planes as a single frontal continuity.

Of course, today we can easily see how Cubism substituted the equally great illusion of a sequence of flat planes of a three-dimensional object, for classical perspective's illusion of depth. These two contradictory modes of optical illusion in fact denote a congruence of representation as the realization of the whole image.

The perspective employed in the fifteenth century supposes the linear transparency of the world and its mastery in unfolding depth to infinity. Thus mankind demonstrates the law of the bipartite division of the universe, of which the painter suggests the image of the whole. From one side, what is manifest is restored to its appropriate human hierarchy, extending to the limits of the infinite, unfathomable, invisible seat of celestial power.

To this conception of representation as the totality of the depth and transparency of the world, Cubism opposes its symmetrical inversion, which will have considerable repercussions on the future of art in the twentieth century.

Now the artist represents totality by synchronizing all possible views of an object, whose three-dimensionality is fragmented in order to be restored in a frontal continuum.

It is both logical and paradoxical to see Giacometti embrace the ideas of the Cubist vision. In the same way that Impressionism was the frame of reference for all new attempts for the generation of 1870, so Cubism, far more than Fauvism, was the obligatory reference point for all young artists who wanted to enter the modern movement after 1913. Giacometti, therefore, involved, in his own way, in the new experiments of his time, would not have been able to ignore the plastic resources of one of the two most important movements since the beginning of the century. It would also seem logical for Giacometti to incorporate into his processes a Cubist vision of the world, whose essence is to represent reality's whole, which he would continue to do although sometimes he produced works that bordered on the Symbolist. Furthermore, the young sculptor's utilizing the theories of Cubism is a fact as paradoxical as the phenomenon of Cubist sculpture itself.

Indeed, if Cubism's central dogma of the synthetic and two-dimensional representation of all the views of an object were adhered to, there could not be any Cubist sculpture in the strict sense. It is quite paradoxical that perception as a procedural method, which proves to be a technique of figural statement whose essential core is the immediate grasp, frontal and entire, of a three-dimensional object, can also be the stylistic technique of a three-dimensional restatement of the representation. Knowing how to dislocate the parts of an object and compress them on a single plane—Cubism's original operative perception expressed in the flat representation of a drawing or painting—was no longer relevant in the three-dimensional world of sculpture. Although Cubist bas-reliefs are easily conceived—Picasso or Laurens have given us wonderful examples—because they integrate into their conception the fundamental principles of total and immediate perception of the additional planes uncovered in the continuity of a new coincidence of parts, given those same fundamental principles, Cubist sculpture is a derivation or a distortion of simple stylistic conformity. Is Cubist sculpture, therefore, a paradoxical proposition, or may one say, without making an extreme paradox, that there is no Cubist sculpture? But it does exist; and from 1925 on, Giacometti would execute his sculptural work within the formal guidelines he had inherited from Cubism.

Furthermore, it seems striking that an artist who always pursued the twin activities of sculpting and painting never produced any pictorial work relating to those tenets of Cubism that he embraced exclusively in the realm of volume. Why did Giacometti choose to take up the aribtrary, twofold contradiction of Cubist sculpture?

In the Cubist representation of an object, carefully taking into account the total breaking down of an object, the artist could not abandon the depth and thickness that would remain, along with the symbolical or psychological elements, a determinant axis of his conception of capturing the world, when most certainly this axis would always lead him to the painful facts of impossibility. But also, in a certain way, the flat Cubist representation, as an attempt take complete account of the entire reality of an object, is a purely realistic mode of representation, which, through its own radicalism, returns to a precise and formal stylistic construction. Giacometti had previously been far too impressed by the irreducibility of emotion and convinced of the reality of the psychological nature of his rapport with the subject to accept this half-measure of a complete description of the subject minus density and emotional interpretation.

On the other hand Cubist sculpture as the product of an arbitrary twofold inversion of reality—a purely mental operation, linguistic, or better yet, a permanent shaping, a style, in the abstract autonomous terms granted it concerning its successive displacements—would be an ideal training ground for the young sculptor who wanted to escape the paralyzing constraints of the model, and the means to attack the fundamental laws of the medium for which he wanted recognition—by constructing a believable volume. Consequently, we should not be too severe toward the Cubist sequence of Giacometti's work and his great dependence on the works of the Cubist masters.

Between 1925 and 1929, after living unhappily with the inadequacy between the latent content with which he wished to invest his work and the form of his reproduction of a subject, Giacometti decided for the time being to renounce the subjective and moral significance he wished to confer on his work, and to address only the realm of pure plastic realization through the medium of an unvarying formal order, a style more than a language. That was the second great achievement of his Cubist period, a corollary to the attainment of the complete expression of his subject, a knowledge of the necessity of conceiving a language appropriate to his desire to convey the whole truth of the model, something which academicism and its stereotypes could not offer him. The question of style, which Giacometti's subsequent work continually asserts, is, first of all, a meditation on the perception of reality, on the sum of the emotive effects on the artist of his obsession with the subject, for which he must acount by an appropriate form.

At the end of his piece on Jacques Callot in 1945, Giacometti delivered his unvarying profession of faith: "But I would like to say once more that in all works of art the subject is of prime importance whether the artist knows it or not. The lesser or greater plastic quality is only the sign of the artist's lesser or greater obsession with his subject; the form is always the measure of that obsession."[1] That is the best definition from the artist's own mouth of the sculptor's deep-rooted, irreducible, and personal rapport with his subject, a rapport that establishes the three intrinsic dimensions of style: perception, interpretation, and plastic statement.

After totality and style, the third great idea manifested in Giacometti's post-Cubist work appears to be a direct derivative of Cubism or of a cultural substratum peculiar to Cubism: primitive African or Oceanic art, whose importance Giacometti would appreciate in a personal way and differently from Picasso and Braque. Magic, or symbolism, comprises this last idea, which Alberto incorporated

42. THE COUPLE (MAN AND WOMAN)
1926 - Bronze, 60 × 37 × 18 cm
Alberto Giacometti Foundation, Zurich

43. LAURENS: CROUCHING NUDE WOMAN (CARYATID)
1934 - Marble, 92 × 44 × 53 cm
Musée national d'Art moderne, Centre Georges Pompidou

into his work by means of his association with Cubism and with ethnography, the latter through his friends Michel Leiris and Georges Henri Rivière.

In the works of the Cubist masters, doubtless Giacometti found the forms of primitive art to be graphic models of radical plastic intensity, of incomparable visual effectiveness; but thanks to his friends, he was well aware of the symbolic significance of primitive art. Its obvious influence on the works of the time is not without importance in the history of the development of the young sculptor's artistic ideas.

First from the impetus of his education and then of his own personality and the deliberate choice of Cézanne as a permanent model, Giacometti always invested his art with the double merit of seeking the correct form, capable of expressing a varied record of feelings, desires, obsessions, and also, later in his mature works, of intellectual and moral choices.

## Torso

Certainly the post-Cubist period represents Giacometti's preeminent interest in formal thought, but in this period the expression of hidden and private content has been separated from the act of creation. (Thus, from 1925 to 1929, the artist continually attempted to reconcile at the same time the synthetic and the disjunctive, the two formal and symbolic categories of his work. *Torso*, 1925 (ill. 44), superbly represents the rigorous integration of stylistic principles of construction by Cubism's angularly circumscribed planes or masses. The influence of Laurens and Lipchitz is obvious, as much from the subject as from the composition. Furthermore, the subject yields to the imperious and precise will of a balance of line and volume.

According to Cézanne, the question here is how to create a harmony parallel with nature but which turns away from any naturalist desire to copy the model. Above all else, *Torso* is an assemblage of cubes. The apex of the thighs shifted from the trunk, thrown back to the edge of the pelvis and bounded by a clean stroke to the upper part of the legs, at the same time accentuates the stylized character of the whole and the triangular structure of the lower part. By this formal contrivance, the sexual symbolism is made evident.

44. GIACOMETTI: TORSO
1925 - Plaster, 57.5 × 25 × 20 cm
Alberto Giacometti Foundation, Zurich

45. SMALL CROUCHING MAN
1926 - Bronze, 28.5 × 17.5 × 10 cm
Alberto Giacometti Foundation, Zurich

## Spoon Woman

If *Torso* of 1925 (ill. 44) is a purely stylistic product of Cubism, *Spoon Woman* of 1926 (ill. 46) is an indirect one. *Spoon Woman* is the result of an assemblage, an idea of construction that would gain much importance several years later in the Surrealist epoch. This idea came directly from the collages and *papiers collés* of Braque and Picasso, and still through the medium of the Cubist aesthetic, represents the first incorporation of Negro art. This sculpture's origin may be found in a remark that Giacometti made about seed scoops shaped like women's bodies, from Oceania and New Guinea. From this first introduction, Giacometti incorporated diverse elements from many sources: between the spoon belly and the breast, the waist is copied from the rolled collar on the necks of Ashanti dolls; the miniaturized head is modeled after Picasso's sculptures in iron, in which the face is sometimes represented by an identifying medallion. *Spoon Woman* is a modern idol; and the size of its belly, placed on a pedestal, oddly surmounted by a cubic breast and a minuscule head, gives authority to this torso and represents very well the emotive and sexual weight attached to this depiction of the artist's idea of femininity as a receptacle, a recipient, with aggressively prominent breasts. The work is a symbolic transposition, in which the power of its construction, through the economical means of Cubism, serves to evoke those erogenous zones.

46. SPOON WOMAN
1926 - Bronze, 145 × 52 × 25 cm
Alberto Giacometti Foundation, Zurich

47. CUBIST COMPOSITION
   1926–27 - Bronze, height 63.5 cm
   Private collection, Zurich

48. PERSONAGES
1926–27 - Bronze, 26 × 20 × 15 cm
Alberto Giacometti Foundation, Zurich

49. THE DANCERS
1927 - Terra cotta, 24 × 17 × 12.5 cm
Musée national d'Art moderne, Centre Georges Pompidou

During these four years of stylistic apprentice-ship, Giacometti realized ten sculptures that lie between the two poles of post-Cubist formalism and the symbolic evocation coming from Negro art, influenced by Lipchitz, Freundlich, Laurens, Archipenko, and sometimes Picasso and Gonzalez. *Small Crouching Man* (1926) (ill. 45), *The Couple* (1926) (ill. 42), *Personages* (1926–1927) (ill. 48), *Reclining Woman* (1929) (ills. 50, 51), *Woman Dreaming* (1929) (ill. 52), and *Man* (1929) (ill. 61) are among creations of this period that integrate sometimes one or the other, sometimes both of those two poles between which the greater part of Giacometti's work swings in those years.

50. RECLINING WOMAN (FRONT VIEW)
   1929 - Plaster, 27 × 44 × 16 cm
   Alberto Giacometti Foundation, Zurich

51. RECLINING WOMAN (THREE-QUARTERS VIEW)
   1929 - Bronze, 27 × 44 × 16 cm

52. WOMAN DREAMING
1929 - Painted bronze, 24.5 × 43 × 14 cm
Alberto Giacometti Foundation, Zurich

### Reclining Woman - Woman Dreaming

These two sculptures, two versions of the same theme, provide the first radical break with vertical construction. Alternating between occupied and empty space, the horizontality of the figures presages the lateral progression of *Woman with Her Throat Cut* (ill. 80). The geometric forms, the simplicity of the articulation give the sculptor the power of access to the force of the symbol, which was the formal force during this period and the basis for the coming Surrealist period.

53. PORTRAIT OF THE ARTIST'S FATHER
1927 - Bronze, 28.5 × 21 × 23 cm
Alberto Giacometti Foundation, Zurich

54. PORTRAIT OF THE ARTIST'S MOTHER
1927 - Bronze, 32.5 × 23 × 11 cm
Alberto Giacometti Foundation, Zurich

55. PORTRAIT OF THE ARTIST'S FATHER (FLAT AND ENGRAVED)
1927 - Bronze, 27.5 × 21.5 × 13.5 cm
Alberto Giacometti Foundation, Zurich

## Portraits of His Father

## Portrait of His Mother

Giacometti's output, still self-taught in character, was parallel and interspersed with his first original works. It is important to note that the sculptor, while involved in the stylistic experiments of his time and his fellow artists, never for a moment abandoned the idea that had so lately met with failure—to make a head. At the end of 1927, he had just completed a portrait of his mother (ill. 54) and two portraits of his father (ills. 53, 55, 56). In these three pieces, especially in the engraved stone head of his father, we can see Alberto's progress toward simplification; the dichotomy between mass and detail is exploited in realizing the concept of the face as at once minimal and expressive. But it is the *Gazing Head* (ill. 62) of 1927 and *Woman* (ills. 59, 60) of 1928 that mark the original development of the artist's work and his first public recognition when these two pieces, also called "flat" sculptures, were exhibited at the Galerie Jeanne Bucher in 1928.

56. PORTRAIT OF THE ARTIST'S FATHER
ca. 1930 - Oil on canvas, 64 × 60 cm
Alberto Giacometti Foundation, Zurich

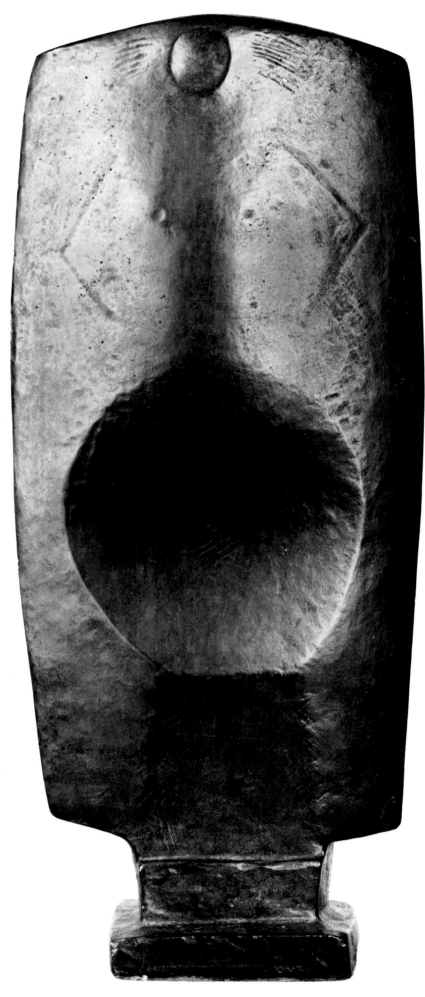

57. WOMAN
1927–28 - Bronze, 39.5 × 16 × 8 cm
Alberto Giacometti Foundation, Zurich

42

58. HEAD
1925 - Plaster, 28.5 × 29.5 × 7.5 cm
Musée national d'Art moderne, Centre Georges Pompidou

### The "Flat" Sculptures

The success with which this series (ill. 57–64) was received by the avant-garde is a measure of the works' originality and Giacometti's mastery of execution. The authority of the idea of his "flat" sculptures rests first of all on the sureness of the stylistic transposition in which bold works are formally simplified. The first presentation of these works completely astounded his contemporaries. This series is, of course, based on the pre-Hellenic statuary of the Cyclades, and was so noted by Christian Zervos in an article devoted to contemporary sculpture in *Cahiers d'art*. But Zervos also observed the subtleties and differences between the appearance of Giacometti's stylistic method and the organic plasticity of the Cycladic idols. "A Cycladic plaque needs only the simplest indications of the form and really embodies all the plastic conditions. Even if one mark were to disappear, the work would never lose its grandeur because each fragment crackles with plasticity; whereas if any part were removed from Giacometti's work now on exhibition [*Man*, Galerie Bernheim, Paris, 1929], one would see that the work would be disorganized by the fact that its unity rests more in its appearance than in its intrinsic plastic qualities." This remark of Zervos' is especially pertinent concerning the female representations in this series: it is their graphic articulation of symbols within a relatively banal framework that controls the plastic presence of the whole. In the same way, in the Gazing Head series, while Giacometti gives us the barest minimum to indicate the face, he gives us a graphic recollection of the subject reproduced.

The series of "flat" sculptures represents the end of the artist's formative period. The problem of the total conception of a work was resolved. Giacometti knew that however subjective the expression of any

43

59. WOMAN
1928 - Bronze, 48 × 38 × 8.5 cm
Alberto Giacometti Foundation, Zurich

60. WOMAN
1928 - Marble, 33.5 × 31 × 9 cm
Alberto Giacometti Foundation, Zurich

motif might be, it needed to be formally and stylistically transposed. He also knew that simple formal manipulation, to which a number of post-Cubist artists had turned, was an unproductive game; thus, he would remain obsessed by his subject and its representation. At twenty-eight, having availed himself of the stylistic teachings of Cubism, Giacometti was freed from what could have been servitude; he was now a sculptor recognized by his peers. Having established the originality of his vision, he could now conceive and realize a new side of his passionate adherence to reality. From 1930 on, at the center of the Surrealist group, he would choose psychic reality as his theme.

1. Alberto Giacometti, "A propos de Jacques Callot," *Labyrinthe* 7 (15 April 1945): 3.

61. MAN (APOLLO)
1929 - Bronze, 40 × 30.5 × 8.5 cm
Alberto Giacometti Foundation, Zurich

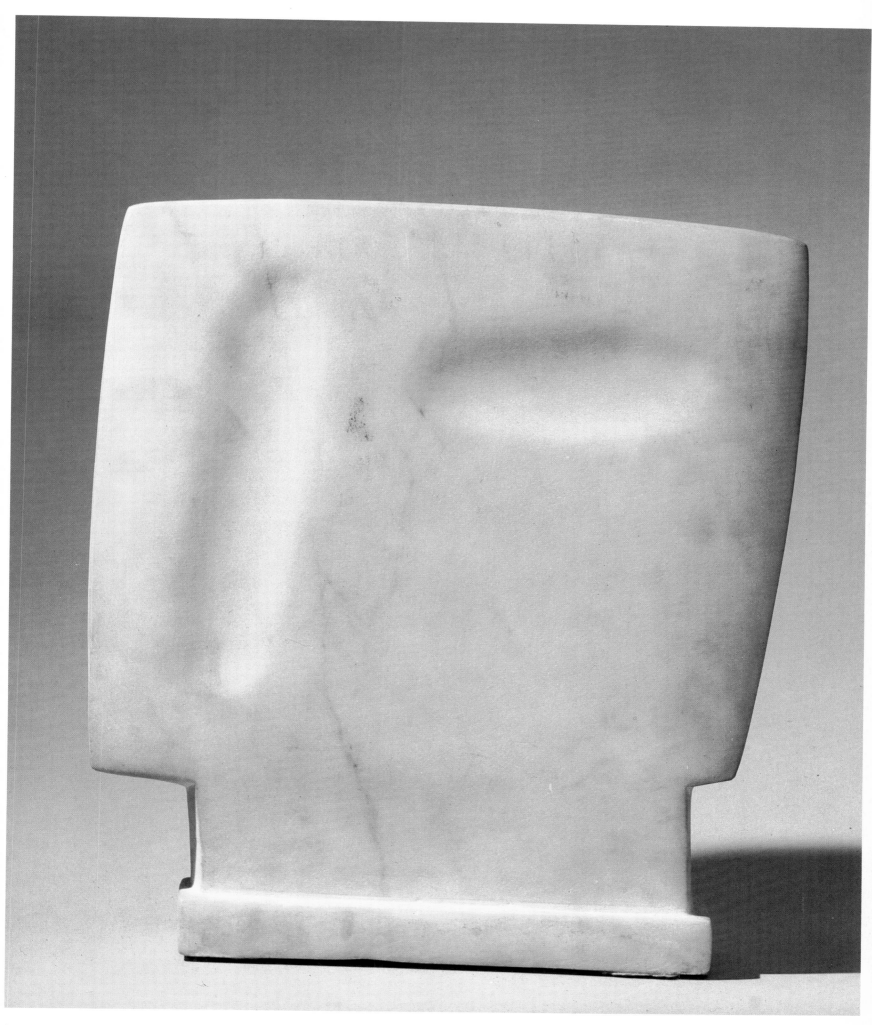

62. GAZING HEAD
1927–29 - Marble, 41 × 37 × 8 cm
Alberto Giacometti Foundation, Zurich

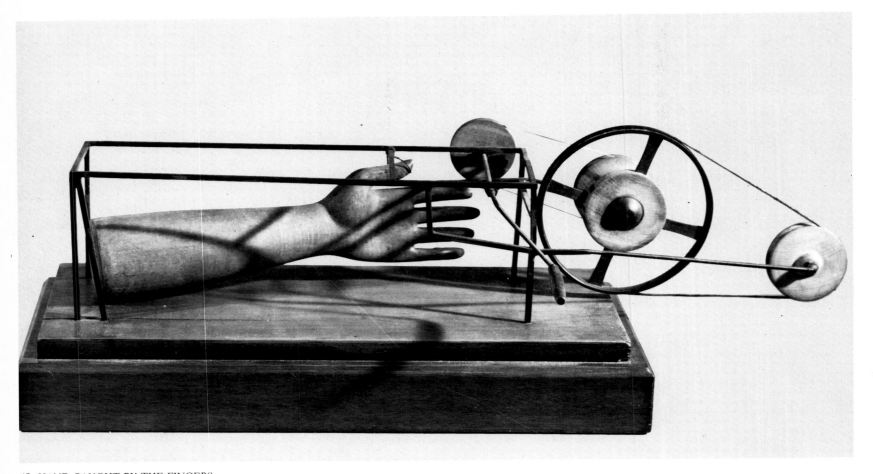

65. HAND CAUGHT BY THE FINGERS
    1932 - Wood and metal, 19 × 59 × 28.5 cm
    Alberto Giacometti Foundation, Zurich

63. MAN
    1925 - Plaster, 48 × 35.3 × 9.5 cm
    Musée national d'Art moderne, Centre Georges Pompidou

64. WOMAN
    1927 - Plaster, 55.3 × 33.1 × 7.8 cm
    Musée national d'Art moderne, Centre Georges Pompidou

# III – The Surrealist Period (1930–1935)

Paradoxically, at the beginning of the twentieth century, it was often in the name of uncompromising realism that the committed avant-garde came to realize the crisis of realism, and to establish the premises of realism from the picture itself and from the practice of art for its own sake. Such ideas would stimulate the development of abstract art.

Neither surrealist art nor Cubist art escaped this ambiguity. In the initial theoretic underpinning imposed by André Breton, Surrealism is an utterly realistic art that, as its name indicates, wishes to break with traditional and academic realism in order to demonstrate the rapport between man and reality. Essentially based on Freudian discoveries, Surrealism was to effect an important transfer, or displacement, point of view, and of the concern, even the primacy, of the work with regard to its subject and its complex relation to reality, the work no longer only the simple statement of this relationship. As Breton also insisted, sometimes vehemently, Surrealism did not want to be an aesthetic movement; formal experimentation is not included in its rules, even though it sometimes occurs in its results. Before being pleasant to look at, a work of Surrealist art must be a significant stratum in a philosophical and anthropological quest.

In the first Surrealist manifesto (1924), André Breton, "once and for all," defined the framework of the movement's activities: "Psychic automatism, through which the real functioning of thought may be expressed either verbally, or in writing, or in any other manner. Dictation of thought completely free from the exercise of reason and exempt from any aesthetic or moral purpose. Surrealism rests on the belief in the superior reality of certain forms of associations neglected until now, in the total power of dreams, and in the impartial play of thought."

Thus Surrealism offered itself as a pure method of impartially recording associations of ideas, or unconscious or subconscious images ordinarily repressed through the censorship of the secondary process of deliberate action. Consequently, dreams, fantasies, desires, sexual impulses—in short, the whole libidinal activity—was to be the center of interest, by the twin claims of the subject's unfettered energy and the representation of his unconscious activity. Surrealist expression, therefore, is a record of the truth of the whole reality of being; and in the subsequent logic of Giacometti's work it is the profound truth of what the mind says (when it does not speak) while transcribing the creative Surrealist act.

Giacometti later affirmed the reason for his ad-herence to Surrealism: "It was the only interesting movement at the time." Precisely so, although we might also mention the totally contradictory importance of the experiments by those artists grouped around the central figure of Mondrian, or of Constantin Brancusi's fine work in the field of sculpture.

However, after the formal freedom Giacometti acquired in the post-Cubist studio, of which the "flat" sculptures mark the crowning achievement, Surrealism represented a return to his habitual preoccupation, that is, the content. He could not be other than attracted by a program that was ordered around a total and radical manifestation of the emotional and philosophical terms of man's general rapport with reality. So it was in the midst of a community of friendship and regard that Giacometti made an only slightly less than triumphant entry into the Surrealist group by showing *The Suspended Ball* (ill. 67), executed between 1930 and 1931, in a Surrealist exhibition. Michel Leiris, André Masson, Georges Limbour, Desnos, Jacques Prévert, Miró, Louis Arogon, Breton, and Salvador Dali were among the earliest admirers of this sculpture, which created a sensation, as much by the force of its symbolic representation of the sexual act as by the introduction of actual movement into sculpture. The piece itself, as Dali has written, became a reference in the plastic experiments of Surrealism: "Objects of symbolic function were envisaged after Giacometti's mute and mobile object, *The Suspended Ball*, an object that lays down and brings together all the essential principles of our definition, but still adheres to the methods of sculpture. Objects of symbolic function leave nothing to formal preoccupations. Corresponding to fantasies and desires plainly stated, they depend only on the amorous imagination and are outside plasticity." Dali's idea is worth quoting for his very apt remark that the Surrealist object has its own sculptural character, as conceived by Giacometti with regard to the formal definition of this same object in Surrealist theory.

In fact, as a Surrealist artist, Giacometti was always and exclusively a sculptor; there were no paintings and very few drawings. We should note the brevity of his stay in André Breton's territory; only five years later in 1935, Giacometti would be excluded from the Surrealists when his interests would once again be purely sculptural. However, his lively formal preoccupations affirm his work as among the best Surrealist sculpture, along with that of Hans Arp and Max Ernst.

66. THE COUPLE (MAN AND WOMAN)
1928–29 - Bronze, 40 × 40 × 16.5 cm
Musée national d'Art moderne, Centre Georges Pompidou

### The Suspended Ball - The Couple

In the famous letter he wrote to Matisse, Giacometti describes *The Suspended Ball* (ill. 67) thus: "A cloven ball suspended in a cage and gliding upon a crescent." This is one of the principal sculptures in the evolution of his work because it contains the direction and orientation of the works executed over the next five years. All the sculptures in the series to which *The Suspended Ball* belongs are enclosed in cubes that Giacometti called "cages." These cages plainly convey closed microcosms in which, according to the sculptor, "transparent constructions" can assert themselves "in a solid mass." He is correct: this is a truly sculptural concept of the interaction between occupied and empty space, which he had already learned in his preceding phase with *Cubist Composition* (ill. 47) and more especially with *Personages* (ill. 48). The artist now took this up again and gave it the density of a geometric presentation of space. The second statement made by *The Suspended Ball*—whose theme would be followed up in other works—concerns the analysis of move-

ment. Regarding this, Giacometti writes: "In spite of all my efforts, I found it impossible to produce a sculpture that gave the illusion of movement—a leg advancing, a raised arm, a head looking sideways. I not only wanted to make it real and effective, I also wanted to give the feeling of causing it."

*The Suspended Ball* certainly satisfies this attempt not merely to illustrate the abstract idea of movement, but to incorporate it as a potential. The dominant feeling is one of a double synchronized movement, the oscillation of the crescent serving as a base for the gliding ball as they intersect. The last statement made by this work, one already undertaken in *Man and Woman* (ill. 66), is an obviously erotic allusion. The suspended movement of the ball on the crescent is a plain metaphorical figure for the sexual act. Picasso, whose influence is obvious in this work, had already signaled in his static realizations the turmoil arising from this same interaction between sphere and crescent.

50

67. THE SUSPENDED BALL
   1930–31 - Plaster and metal, 61 × 36 × 33.5 cm
   Alberto Giacometti Foundation, Zurich

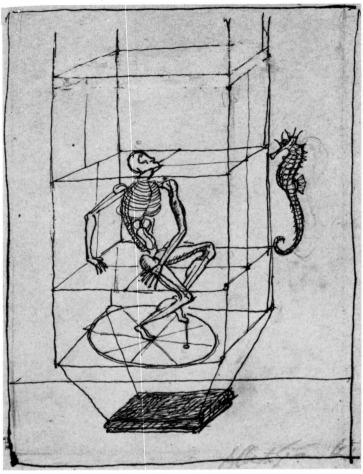

68. FEET IN A DISH
1933 - Pen drawing, 12.3 × 8.8 cm
Kupferstichkabinett, Kunstmuseum, Basel

## The Cage

The scenography of *The Suspended Ball* is repeated in *The Cage* (ill. 71), carried out in wood and endowed with a different meaning and more complex in its internal structure. We have the same closed microcosm in which coincidences and oppositions confront one another in the kind of organic theater in which the Surrealists delighted. Faithful to his conception of art, in *The Cage*, Giacometti created a synthesis of existential vision in a confined battleground on which lie the broken remains of the tragic masculine-feminine combat.

This world of cruelty and suffering, of dismemberment, seems at first sight to belong to the classic subject matter of the Surrealists; for example, they honored Sade as a precursor. Antonin Artaud, Georges Bataille, and Michel Leiris have all glorified the complex relations between cruelty, death, and sex in their writings; and it seems likely, given the recurrence of these themes in Giacometti's work, that he found there an outlet for his own obsessions. It cannot be doubted that the close friendship between those who worked on the review *Documents*, in particular Leiris and Bataille, had a decisive influence at that time on Giacometti's stylistic and philosophical ideas.

69. SURREALIST DRAWING
ca. 1932 - Pen drawing, 31 × 23.8 cm
Musée national d'Art moderne, Centre Georges Pompidou

70. THE CAGE
1930–31 - Pencil drawing, 13.6 × 12.2 cm
Musée national d'Art moderne, Centre Georges Pompidou

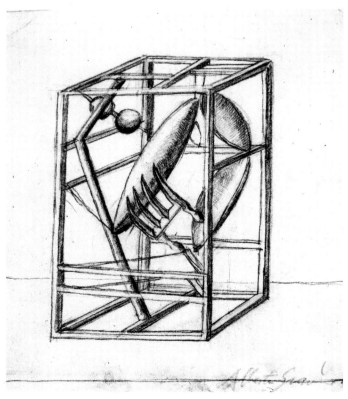

71. THE CAGE
1930–32 - Wood, 49 × 26.5 × 26.5 cm
Moderna Museet, Stockholm

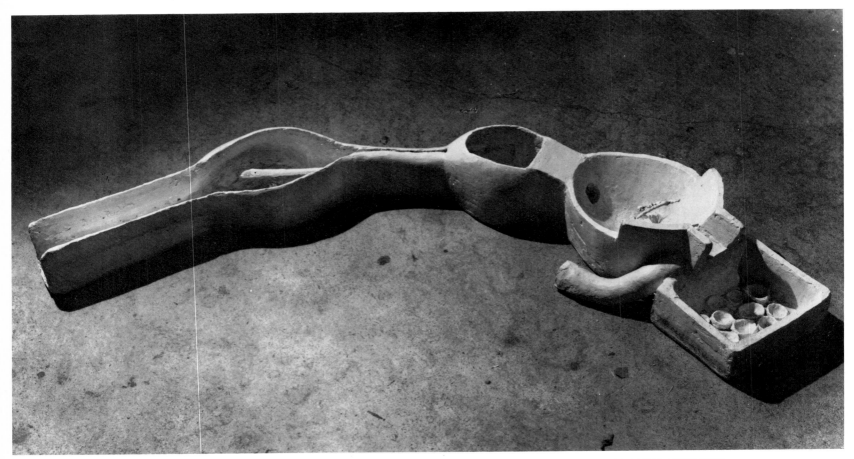

72. DESIGN FOR A CORRIDOR (THE LABYRINTH)
1930–31 - Plaster, 16 × 125 × 42 cm
Alberto Giacometti Foundation, Zurich

### Design for a Corridor - Woman with Her Throat Cut - Unpleasant Object for Throwing - Man, Woman, and Child

*Design for a Passage* (ill. 72), retitled by the artist in 1947 *Design for a Corridor*, makes use of the same bizarre inspiration, although very different in appearance. Sometimes also called *The Labyrinth*, this work in plaster is an obvious allusion to the cervical passage. During those years the theatrical form of the artist's subconscious and unconscious desires became the subject of his work, a serial succession that explored all the modalities of sculptural fantasy.

With *The Suspended Ball*, then *The Cage, Point to the Eye, Hand Caught by the Fingers, Flower in Danger*, the series Unpleasant Objects (ills. 65, 67, 71, 75–79), to *The Tormented Woman in Her Room at Night*, and above all with the masterpiece *Woman with Her Throat Cut* (1932) (ill. 80), Giacometti put together a huge repertoire of repellent themes and subjects. Over this important assemblage he distilled the essence of his tragic vision, always dominated by forms of cruelty, emptiness, murder and torture, always constructed on a sexual and sadomasochistic base.

Another important period might be called the Topographies of Desire, consisting of works that Giacometti presented in the form of planes or spaces invested with the capacity to represent destiny and desire. They were in accord with a subject dear to the Surrealists—the symbolic representation of that internal reality between life and death, desire and the law. *Design for a Corridor* (ill. 72); *No More Play*; *Man, Woman, and Child* (ill. 73); *Circuit*; *Design for a Sculpture* (ill. 74) document this particular series.

However it is viewed, Giacometti's vision is dominated by the same black crest. Existence is a battlefield of mortal conflict, the outcome determined by sexual desire. Destiny is like a billiard ball condemned to roll eternally without ever finding a stopping place, a resting place, or any stability whatever, in the groove of its endless wanderings. It was not simply under the influence of Surrealism that Giacometti thus created an oeuvre in the form of a great symbolic dramaturgy. Surrealism gave only a momentary technical and theoretical authorization to confront that theme, which gave

54

73. MAN, WOMAN, AND CHILD
1931 - Wood and metal, 41.5 × 37 × 16 cm
Kunstmuseum, Basel. Gift of Arp-Hagenbach

74. DESIGN FOR A SCULPTURE
1931 - Pen drawing, 22 × 18 cm
Alberto Giacometti Foundation, Zurich

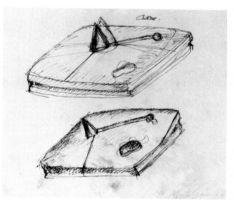

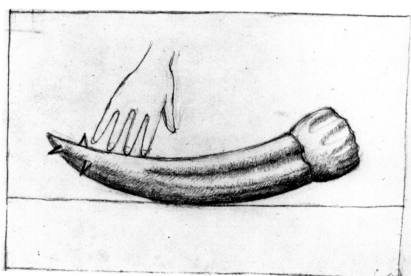

75. UNPLEASANT OBJECT FOR THROWING
1931 - Bronze, 22 × 30 × 28.5 cm
Alberto Giacometti Foundation, Zurich

76. UNPLEASANT OBJECT
1931-32 - Pencil Drawing, 9 × 14 cm
Musée national d'Art moderne, Centre Georges Pompidou

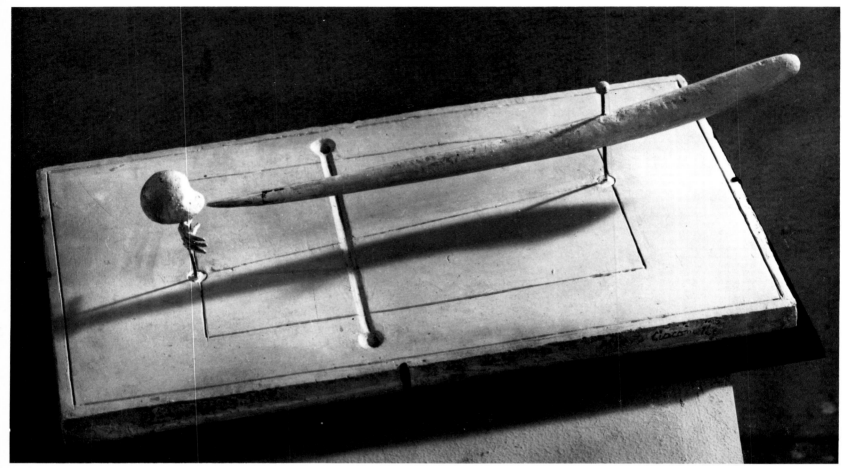

77. POINT TO THE EYE
1931 - Plaster and metal, 12 × 59 × 30 cm
Alberto Giacometti Foundation, Zurich

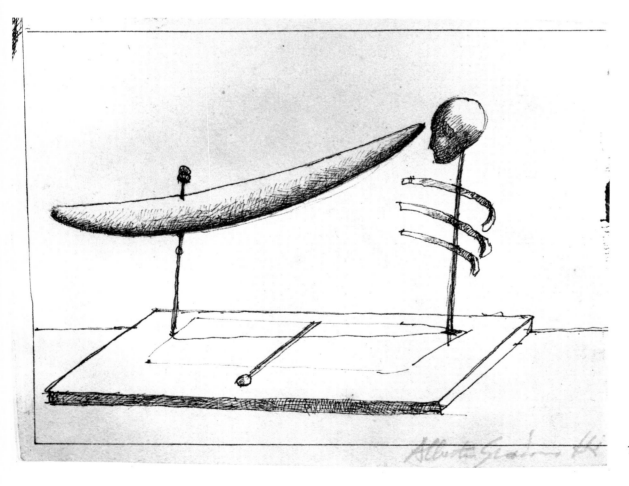

78. POINT TO THE EYE
1931 - Pencil drawing
Alberto Giacometti Foundation, Zurich

79. FLOWER IN DANGER
   1933 - Wood, metal, and plaster, 55.5 × 78.5 × 18 cm
   Alberto Giacometti Foundation, Zurich

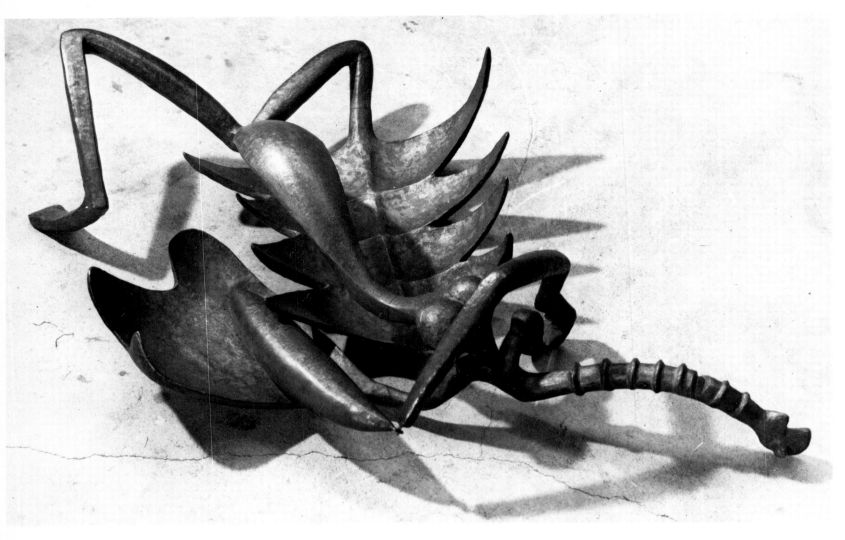

80. WOMAN WITH HER THROAT CUT
1932 - Bronze, 20 × 75 × 58 cm
Alberto Giacometti Foundation, Zurich

81. LAURENS: ONDINES
1933 - Bronze, 80 × 160 cm
Musée national d'Art moderne, Centre Georges Pompidou

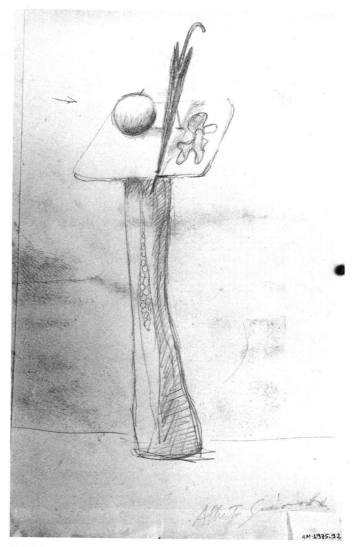

82. WOMAN WITH HER THROAT CUT
1932 - Pencil and ink drawing, 33.4 × 22 cm
Musée national d'Art moderne, Centre Georges Pompidou

83. WOMAN WITH HER THROAT CUT
1932 - Pencil drawing, 33.4 × 22 cm
Musée national d'Art moderne, Centre Georges Pompidou

logic and continuity to his whole work—the representation by all possible means of a vision of total life.

The two great works that close this important period *The Palace at 4 A.M.* (1932) (ill. 88) and *The Table* (1933) (ill. 91) are good examples of Giacometti's genius for interposing himself between an enigmatic figure and a vision of the revelation of the dramaturgy of existence. These two works are at first sight scenography, but they are also above all recapitulations. *The Palace* summarizes and synthesizes the knowledge and emotions experienced by Giacometti in Surrealist circles; while in the following year *The Table* summarizes and synthesizes his knowledge of form. *The Palace* is an enclosed synthesis, while *The Table* is an open and

projecting recapitulation, in which the earlier stylistic formulations already serve the intention of the Surrealist period. In writing about Giacometti, it is usual to admit, in the diachronic evaluation of his work, that the Surrealist period was prolonged until 1935, with the celebrated sculpture *The Invisible Object* (ill. 101) marking its end, due no doubt to André Breton's interest in it. This division is arguable; it would seem that, on the contrary, the recapitulative works such as *The Palace* and *The Table* might well be considered the conclusive end of this period.

Those works which appeared between 1933 and 1935 already belong to a new sequence whose object was a more formal approach, a return to reality.

84. PALAIS A QUATRE HEURES DE L'APRÈS-MIDI
1932 - Dessin à l'encre, 21,5 × 27 cm
Museum of Modern Art, New York.

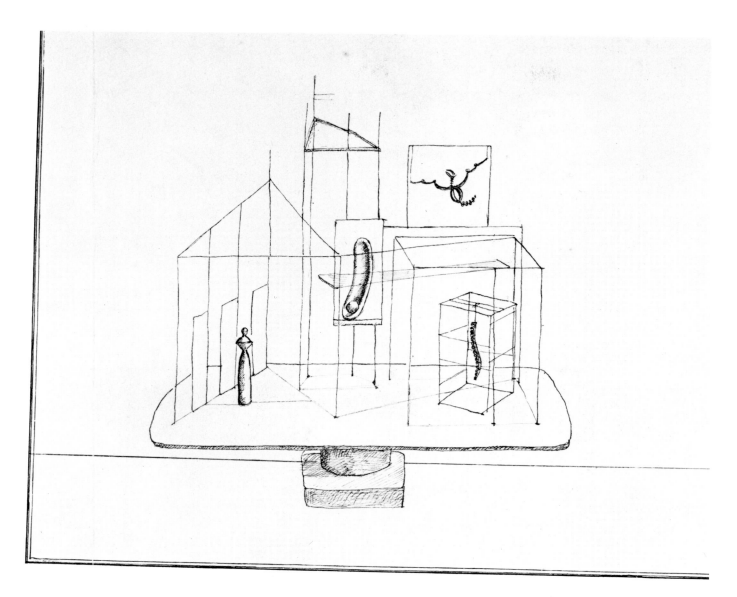

85. THE PALACE AT 4 A.M.
1932 - Pen drawing, 19.2 × 24.3 cm
Kupferstichkabinett, Kunstmuseum, Basel

## The Palace at 4 A.M.

Together with a few other masterpieces, *The Palace at 4 A.M.* (ill. 88) is a construction whose effect was decisive in establishing Giacometti's fame and which marks the importance of his contribution to the Surrealist movement. Both a synthesis and a marvelous enigma, *The Palace*, as its title indicates, is a nocturnal vision, a dramatic, dreamlike composition containing multiple scenes which identify Giacometti's main themes—women, death, dreams. These themes are set in a theatrical space and at a distance, which reveals their central, absolute value as an enigma. The most elaborate development of the whole Cage series, *The Palace*, through its spatial ambivalence of the closed microcosm and the open stage, represents more than the simple expres-

sion of confinement and the tragedy of imprisonment.

This work has multiple roots. Reinhold Hohl has noted theatrical influences in its construction. It particularly echoes the reproduction of a stage model from the Meyerhold Theater in Moscow, derived from Tairov's decor for *L'Orage*, by Ostrovsky, which the artist knew from a photograph.

Reinhold Hohl also observes that the appearance of the female figure in the forground of the raised rectangles, on the left, might have been conceived while recollecting one of Giovanni Giacometti's paintings, *Les Porteuses de pierre de Promontogno* (ill. 86), but this arrangement also recalls the artist's first memory of his mother standing before a cur-

61

tain. Undoubtedly, in his inspiration for the conception of *The Palace*, Giacometti employed his memory of a picture much appreciated by the Surrealists, Arnold Böcklin's *L'Île des morts* (ill. 87), in the Kunstmuseum in Basel. There is a simple transposition from left to right between the two representations. In Böcklin's work, the three openings to the tombs are placed beneath a rocky triangular dome on the right; while in *The Palace* they appear on the left as vertical rectangles behind the female figurine and surmounted by the triangular pediment of the palace. In the picture, on the left, the cubic shape of the Chapel of the Dead crowned by an irregular rocky parallelogram becomes in *The Palace* the tiered and roofed cubic spaces in which Giacometti has hung a vertebral column, a bird's skeleton above it. The cypress trees in the center of the picture become the dominant central poles of *The Palace*. The central figure halfway up the poles of the tower, with whom Giacometti identified him-

87. BÖCKLIN: L'ÎLE DES MORTS
1880 - Oil on canvas, 111 × 155 cm
Kunstmuseum, Basel

self, is seen in the luminous light of the landing stage of *L'Île des morts*.

Finally, the female figurine representing the artist's mother is modeled on Böcklin's veiled feminine figure in the boat in the composition's foreground. Even the base of *The Palace* reminds us of the sea surrounding *L'Île des morts*. Beyond this astonishing mixture of sources, in whose content the essence of Giacometti's active inspiration has been concentrated, he has stressed the personal and autobiographical allusions in this work. *The Palace* was conceived and created as a dream, the elements of daily existence condensed and shifted through the prism of the artist's thoughts and emotions. Between the mother and life and death, the subject is suspended and enclosed. This basically unchanging vision of life, or general existence, which is set in the middle of the insurmountable contradiction between Eros and Thanatos, is revealed in *The Palace* and exercises a powerful fascination over the viewer.

Quite apart from the formal quality and admirable clarity of the plastic conception of this work, its categorical importance is that of a definitive proof, a record and synthesis, of the author's psyche.

In *The Palace* Giacometti understood his subject once and for all; but he also understood his craft; and the following year *The Table* would offer proof of this.

86. GIOVANNI GIACOMETTI: LES PORTEUSES
DE PIERRE DE PROMONTOGNO
1895–96 - Oil on canvas, 280 × 200 cm
Musée de Coire

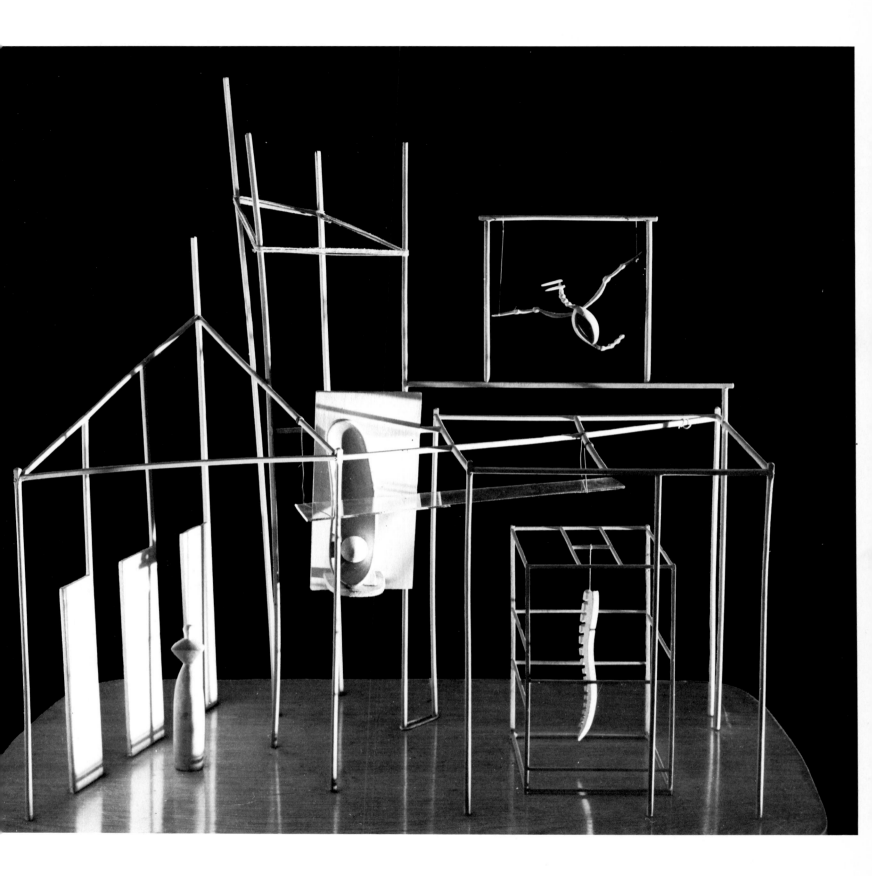

88. THE PALACE AT 4 A.M.
1923 - Wood, glass, metal, string, 62.5 × 70.6 × 39.5 cm
Museum of Modern Art, New York

89. THE SURREALIST TABLE
   1933 - Chinese ink drawing, 23.5 × 20 cm
   Musée national d'Art moderne, Centre Georges Pompidou

90. THE SURREALIST TABLE
   ca. 1930 - Pen drawing, 6.1 × 7.4 cm
   Kupferstichkabinett, Kunstmuseum, Basel

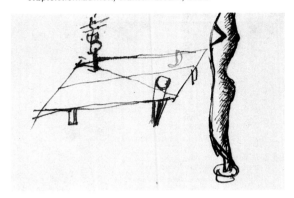

## The Table

In one way *The Table* (ills. 89–92) is a commissioned work. It was created with the idea in mind of an exhibition of Surrealist objects at the Galerie Pierre Colle in June of 1933. The work represents the same attempt as the synthesis that presided over the development of *The Palace*—but now on a formal plane—and offers a conclusive statement of the stylistic material at the sculptor's disposal. Thus, it's no accident that we observe woven into this sculpture's composition a perfect mastery of the two great influences of Giacometti's formal thought—Cubism and Surrealism. *The Table* is a retrospective work, which at the same time acknowledges the artist's debts to some of the best of his contemporaries.

We are concerned then with a work full of "quotations," one whose cohesiveness is assured by a scenic definition of the whole much to the Surrealist taste, but we should not also neglect the complex web of allusions aimed at a symbolic explanation of the artist's spiritual state. He was, at this point in his career, revising wholesale his methods in order to make manifest the irreducible dimension of his personal world vision.

The Surrealist *The Table* carries two major references: one is *The Difficult Crossing* (1926) (ill. 93), painted by René Magritte, and the other is Fernand Léger's series Déjeuners à table (1920–1922) (ill. 97).

From Magritte's work, Giacometti kept the table with legs that do not match and which has a severed hand upon it—this last motif had also appeared in works by Chirico and Max Ernst. The right front table leg pays subtle homage to the Constantin Brancusi work *The Endless Column* (1918). Finally, Giacometti borrows again from Magritte's picture *The Two Sisters*, from which he takes the female bust, as well as the curtain or veil behind the table, which he uses to half-obscure the figure's face, an idea already employed by Fernand Léger.

The small vase on the table top is also taken from Léger's compositions from the early twenties that use the theme of the lunch table. In addition, Giacometti has also placed a polyhedron on the table—he employed a new version in 1934—which further affirms the influence of Brancusi's artistic ideas.

With this work, therefore, Giacometti clearly marked out the divisions and the stakes among the aesthetic formulations he had confronted, to which in a large measure he owed his success. But it would be unfair to narrow this important work to a simple stylistic formula of debts owed or paid, or to formal uncertainties. Whatever mastery it displays, its fascination lies first and foremost in the enigma it offers us. If its appellation "Surrealist Table" is well merited, and if it belongs to the finest inheritance from that movement, it is because it offers us a web

91. THE TABLE
1933 - Plaster, 148 × 103 × 43 cm
Musée national d'Art moderne, Centre Georges Pompidou

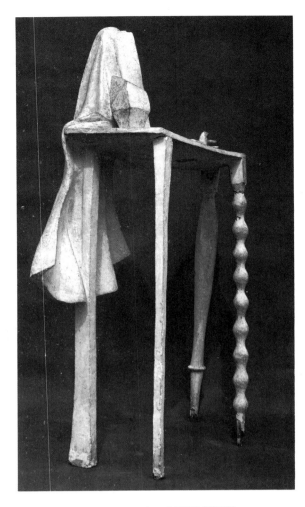

92. THE TABLE (THREE-QUARTERS VIEW)

93. MAGRITTE: LA TRAVERSÉE DIFFICILE
1926 - Oil on canvas, 80 × 65.3 cm
Private collection

of its own symbolic associations and of its creator's hidden thoughts. Its dramaturgy and the care bestowed on its composition are not immaterial to the question of meaning and its development, in which lies one of the essential points of Giacometti's artistic ideas.

In this construction of a dramatic edifice halfway between everyday things and art, Giacometti gives us a key to his vision. This table, placed between the grasp of reality and the abstraction of art, is in itself a manifestation of the artist's position of reconciliation. Consequently, this piece places first the artist and then the viewer at the crossroads of the two great spheres that determine the disposition of this sculpture: art or reality, art and reality. There is a strong feeling of opposing forces between the abstract figure of the polyhedron, identifiable at once as a sculpture and as art, and the severed hand, originating from the earlier sculpture of *Hand Caught by the Fingers* (ill. 65). Between the concentrated mass of the polyhedron and the hand with open fingers and raised thumb, Giacometti has set the figure, or rather the effigy, of a woman veiled and unveiled. We may also notice that it is far from unimportant in the composition of the sculpture that the veil, the lowered curtain over the woman's face, is on the same side as the polyhedron. In contrast, the open eye, or rather that one-eyed stare, is on the side of the hand. If the sculpture is viewed in this way, it appears as if Giacometti has actually

94. THE TABLE (DETAIL)

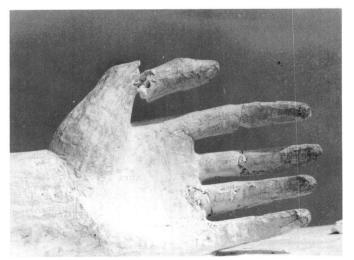

66

traced the line of the veil to mark not only differentiation but opposition, which also denote the ambivalence of the face itself and of the enigma that it represents.

If we believe, as seems reasonable, that Giacometti's Surrealist work—most especially the series Unpleasant Objects to which *Hand Caught by the Fingers* belongs—reflects the artist's personal emotions, then the hand on the Surrealist table represents that of the artist and the power of his creative act. However, this power is a tragic one, which forbids a formal and abstract execution of the work and proceeds instead to amputation and symbolic castration. Here the whole theory of sublimation seems to be in operation, for the artist must in some way renounce a large part of himself for art, and in Giacometti's case, for woman, and for the troubling, ambivalent insistence of his vision.

As envisaged by Giacometti, who identified with the very essense of art, the artist's work is to veil and unveil the invisibility of woman, an invisibility in the deepest meaning of the word, through which she looks at the artist and establishes the reality of the art.

Thus, the hand placed within the woman's one-eyed gaze seems to show—in fact, to point to—the artist's ulterior purpose: a reality that the hand would so often try to model on the very body of a woman.

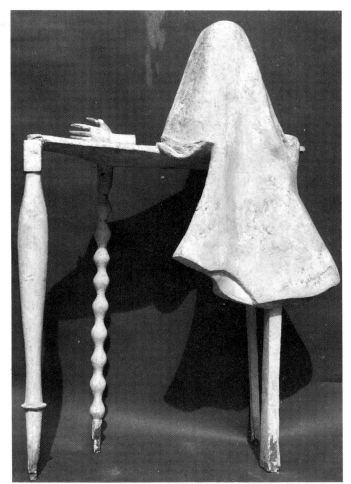

96. THE TABLE (BACK VIEW)

97. LÉGER: LE PETIT DÉJEUNER
(Study for *Les Déjeuners*)
1921 - Oil on canvas, 92 × 65 cm
Musée national d'Art moderne, Centre Georges Pompidou

95. THE TABLE (DETAIL)

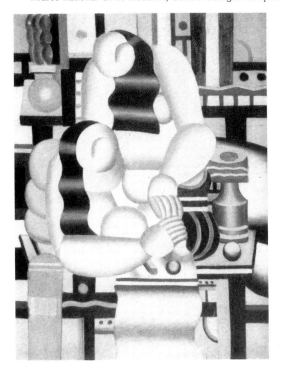

98. THE CARESS (IN SPITE OF THE HANDS)
1932 - Marble, 40 × 37 × 11 cm
Musée national d'Art moderne, Centre Georges Pompidou

# IV – The Period of Transition and Maturation (1932–1939)

As already stated, there is always an artificial delimitation that creeps into a body of work, dividing it rigidly into consecutive periods, while at the same time claiming to describe and characterize it by this method.

Thus, between 1932 and 1939 Giacometti's work seems to be a tissue of differentiated and sometimes contradictory choices. The various experiments that he pursued, based on the provisional conclusions of *The Palace* and *The Table*, tend to make us think that during these eight years, he went through a period of transition and maturation, which led to his personal and definitive style. Although critics of Giacometti's work agree that the final and finest achievement of his Surrealist period is *The Invisible Object* (ill. 101), for the reality of the diachronic variation of its component parts; as early as 1932, the sculptor already had many times deviated from Surrealist dogma in order to experiment in areas other than those marked out by André Breton and his group.

## The Caress

Therefore the marble work entitled *The Caress* (ill. 98) of 1932 seems to fit the Surrealist objectives. First called *In Spite of the Hands*, it attempts to condense several themes into a single continuum of form. Undoubtedly, it betrays some marginal influences of Arp and Brancusi, but, more importantly, the work's meaning lies in its subject. A stylized conception, with lowered head and procreative, feminine belly embraced by masculine hands, this sculpture, based on a distillation of heterogenous traits, tends toward the construction of an anamorphosis, an optical phenomenon in which Giacometti's followers evinced great interest, and which would also, according to Jean Clair, be the subject of the Surrealistic *Point to the Eye* (ill. 77). An anamorphosis realizes in a representation the often veiled introjection of a figure, sometimes hardly discernible at first glance, which is sometimes the profound truth of the representation, sometimes its structure, often its focus. Holbein's famous picture *The Ambassadors* remains the model for this device, in which in the center of the picture, crossing the painting, an oblong form—a skull—is set in the middle of the diplomats' reunion. In *The Caress*, Giacometti has used a similar method of constructing the image. Though at first glance it looks like a "head-landscape," the underlying theme, in fact, is

that of conception, of childbirth and femininity, placed between the impression of a man's hands. The true subject of this sculpture, conception, will again be treated, although quite differently, in 1935 in *1 + 1 = 3*.

## 1 + 1 = 3

In this latest work (ill. 99), it is the structure itself that is the symbolic support of the woman's body. The title is explicit: the joining of the phallus with the female body. In *The Caress* and *1 + 1 = 3*, Giacometti again discovered in a roundabout way the central inspiration of his work, which in the years 1932 to 1939 would constitute a decisive approach: the reality of the human body and, more particularly, the representation of woman. We have said that this was a period of transition and maturing; it was also marked by the artist's temporary political commitment to the Marxist revolution. Under the pseudonym of Ferrache, Giacometti did satirical sketches for Aragon's and Georges Sadoul's publication *La Lutte*.

During this same period, faced with the necessity of providing for his material existence, Giacometti collaborated in somewhat artistic undertakings. He designed jewelry for Schiaparelli and Lelong; with his brother Diego, he created décors and furniture; and crowning his efforts to feed himself, he collabo-

99. 1 + 1 = 3
1935 - Plaster
Private collection

rated with the scene-painter Jean-Michel Frank. These years, therefore, seem in essence contradictory to us: on one hand, he was involved in social and political struggle and on the other, he was providing services and amenities to the wealthy international bourgeoisie.

On the artistic plane, he had absorbed the best teachings of Cubism and the philosophical and anthropoligical opportunities of Surrealism; and he could not or would not choose to limit himself to one of the two great artistic orders then reigning in Paris.

Visiting the Louvre with Pierre Schneider, Giacometti confided some of the thoughts that he would later have occasion to articulate many times to those whom he would meet: "Realism is a lot of rubbish. . . . What we call the great styles in art are those that approach most closely the vision one has of things. Yes, those works of the past that I find most resembling reality are generally judged to be the farthest from it. I mean the arts of style: Chaldean, Egyptian, Byzantine, Fayumic, Chinese things, Christian miniatures of the high Middle Ages. . . . For me, Egyptian painting is realist painting, although they call it the most stylized. Anyone among us resembles much more an Egyptian sculpture than any other kind of sculpture ever made. . . . That's the style that gives us the truest vision."[1]

In that decade before the war, Giacometti's principal works were inspired by the necessity he felt to express human representation in the preliminary form of a stylistic act. In these works, Giacometti first valued his ability to render the general reality of a body. Also, Giacometti acknowledged that through the intervention of the concept of style, the symbolic significance, spirituality, or mystery of a figure cannot be a supra-added dimension, easily manipulated by a will determined at random; but as Egyptian art teaches, that the symbolic dimension is an intrinsic effect on the stylistic formation of the figure.

## Walking Woman

If *The Mannequin* (1933) is another concession to Surrealism and echoes the humorous line from Man Ray's famous photograph *Le Violon d'Ingres* (1924), the *Nude*, worked on from 1932 to 1934, or the *Walking Woman* (1934) (ill. 100), elegant statues that might be termed classical, introduced into the artist's work a new timeless dimension and the stylized proportion of Egyptian statuary to which Giacometti had already explicitly referred, though he was encouraged, it is true, by Archipenko's works. In this short series that ends with the masterpiece *The Invisible Object* (ill. 101), Giacometti's return to reality is first of all a return to the

100. WALKING WOMAN
1932–33 - Bronze, height 151 cm
Private collection

anthropometric dimension of his creations, but, also, obviously shows his persistence in the representation of the female body. Nevertheless, in these works of numerous heterogenous elements, there exists a desire to submit to what one sees. The absence of head and arms is obviously an important concession to academic statuary and concedes a willingness to portray a classical fragment. But we may notice that these two statues (*The Mannequin* and *Walking Woman*) are stamped with a shallow, triangular cavity in the chest. This concession is of a symbolic order and signifies that the maker felt the need to offer the symbolic trace or intention of content, however residually.

## The Invisible Object

Thanks to the account that André Breton relates in *L'Amour fou*, we have some notes on Giacometti's difficulties with this piece (ill. 101), which give the orthodox Surrealist interpretation that Breton could not fail to give us.

Breton considered this work to be "for the emanation of the desire to love and be loved, in search of its true objective and in its unhappy ignorance" to be the highest and most complex achievement of this period. Also titled *Hands Holding the Void*, this statue is both fascinating and enigmatic.

Taking an Oceanic ancestor as a model, Giacometti added, with the characteristic placement of the hands held before the breast, the identical structure of the presentation of the sacred object of Isis by the Queen Caromama, an Egyptian statue that he had copied. Similarly, it is to Egyptian statuary that Giacometti owes the plank that hides the lower part of the legs.

Beyond this sculpture's inventory of references, it is its supernatural force of expression, the imperial way in which it draws our gaze toward the mystery of the invisible that confers the mantle of divinity on this figure. Perhaps this figure, with the upper part projected and the lower impeded, is also a powerful metaphor of life today. Such a division was doubtless experienced by Giacometti, whose endeavors drew him toward the visible, but were obstructed by emptiness and despair. Such an epoch of man is symbolized by the bird placed on the chair beside the personage.

## The Cube - Cubist Heads

It is from this same period that we can date Giacometti's return to the head in sculpture, foreshadowed by the Surrealist *The Table* in the form of an abstract polyhedron. Entitled *The Cube* (1934) (ill. 102), this work constitutes in some way a transition to the theme that continually haunted the

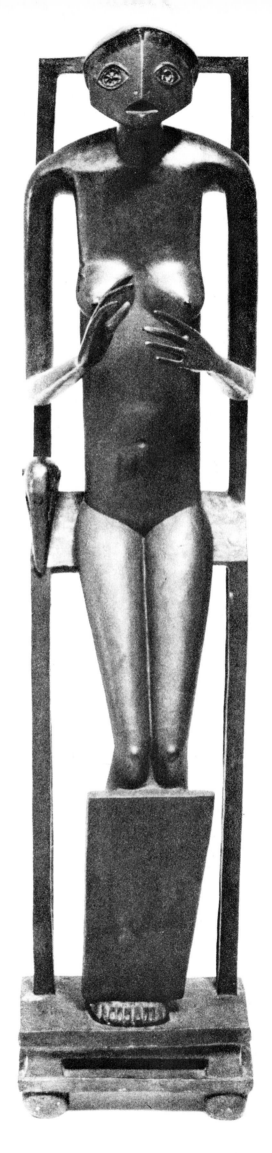

101. THE INVISIBLE OBJECT
1934-35 - Bronze, height 153 cm
Maeght Foundation, Saint-Paul-de-Vence

102. THE CUBE
1934 - Bronze, 94 × 60 × 60 cm
Alberto Giacometti Foundation, Zurich

103. CUBIST HEAD
1934 - Plaster, 18 × 19 × 21 cm
Alberto Giacometti Foundation, Zurich

104. CUBIST HEAD
1934 - Plaster, height 20 cm
Private collection, New York

sculptor and that he anticipates once again. In *The Cube* and both pieces titled *Cubist Head* (ills. 103, 104), it is still the constructive idea of the representation of cranial volume that predominates. The artist did not seek the expression of a head's reality, but rather its formal value, which led him back to the great theme that had absorbed him. It was at this stage (late 1934, early 1935) that Giacometti envisaged a return to the model, though in a very transitory way. Thus, he explains in his famous letter to Pierre Matisse: "Then I wanted to make compositions with figures. For that I had to do one or two life studies (quickly), just enough to understand the construction of a head, of the whole figure, and in 1935 I hired a model. These studies took me about a fortnight, I think, and then I resolved to make my compositions."

What he believed to be nothing more than a two-week interlude would turn out to be his life's work. From 1935 on, Giacometti had found the challenging path that he would follow until his death in 1966.

The first consequence of these new aesthetic and moral intentions, which distanced him equally from the tumult of the avant-garde and the social and political struggle, was his exclusion from the Surrealist group by Breton, who exclaimed: "A head! Everybody knows what a head is!" Having simultaneously lost a good number of his friends and the support of the dealers, the artist, like his master Cézanne, worked out his subject in absolute solitude. In this motif he found the same overwhelming feeling of impotence that had similarly seized him some years earlier.

As the sculptor was to declare many times, during this period there was no question of his returning to academic naturalism; rather, his aim was to form a stylistic foundation whose amplitude and plastic relevance would allow him to include and address the question of reality. For the five years preceding 1940, Giacometti's difficulties were the result of a deficiency and even a contradiction between the handling of the general configuration of the subject and the scattering of the details, which he could not succeed in incorporating into the structure of the whole. As he has said: "In the beginning I saw nothing. . . . Nothing was as I imagined it. I could only distinguish innumerable details. . . . The more I looked at the model, the thicker the screen between myself and reality."

That screen of which he spoke is certainly the autonomous reality of plastic language that denotes and renders the subject, while obstructing its actual meaning. The problem posed by this radical confrontation between the sculptor and his model remains the discovery of a form and style whose capacity to synthesize the entirety of the details noted by the artist will endow a work of art with a power equal to that of the reality that inspired it. When Giacometti declares, emphasizing the helplessness of his position, "You begin by seeing the model, but little by little all the possible sculptures get in the way," he gets to the heart of the problem: the irreducible density that represents the statement, as opposed to the multiplicity of all other possible statements that denote the same reality. He described the experience that led him to zero degree of representation, to the exclusion of all knowledge and presupposition, in the rigor of annihilation: "There were too many sculptures between me and my model. And when there were no more sculptures, there was an unknown, so that I no longer knew whom or what I saw."

## Diego - Rita - The Egyptian (Isabel)

These prewar years are crucial to the formation of Giacometti's thought and to the adjustment of those ideas that would hold sway over the development of his future work. Undoubtedly, the works created at this time, the heads of Diego, Rita (ill. 106), and *The Egyptian* (or *Isabel*, ill. 105) do not display very well that decisive evolution in the sculptor's thought. They are sufficiently academic, without any particular enhancement; and their importance lies much more in the implied necessity of Giacometti finding a new solution to his problems than in their being masterly accomplishments arising from various stages of this thought.

106. BUST OF RITA
1938 - Bronze, height 22 cm
Kunsthaus, Zurich

105. THE EGYPTIAN (ISABEL)
1936 - Bronze, height 29 cm
Private collection

## Apple on the Sideboard

## The Artist's Mother

In 1937 he did two paintings, *Apple on the Sideboard* (ill. 110) and *The Artist's Mother* (ill. 107), important pictures in that they already bore the components of his future pictorial work. Although these paintings are successful in that they seize our attention, they are abortive acts in view of the artist's preoccupations during this period and the profound crisis that led him to stop exhibiting until 1947.

107. THE ARTIST'S MOTHER
1937 - Oil on canvas, 61 × 50 cm
Pierre Matisse collection, New York

108–109.  DRAWINGS FROM "MY STUDIO"
1932 - Pencil drawings, each 32 × 49 cm
Kupferstichkabinett, Kunstmuseum, Basel

110. APPLE ON THE SIDEBOARD
1937 - Oil on canvas, 74 × 76.5 cm
Pierre Matisse collection, New York

## Miniature Sculptures

(Original size reproduced)

111. MAN ON A PEDESTAL
1940–41 - Bronze, height 8.4 cm
Private collection

112. WOMAN'S HEAD ON A PEDESTAL
1945–46 - Bronze, height 12 cm
Private collection

113. ARMLESS FIGURE
1946–47 - Bronze, height 12 cm
Private collection

When he placed himself in the frame of the frontal relationship with his model, Giacometti discovered the insurmountable distance separating them; he also perceived that the duration of the process must be incorporated into the formation of the figure if he was to render the absolute reality of his position as observer of a model placed in the enigma of distance itself. The distance between himself and the model not only was soon to be a plastic given, inherent in the sculptor's work, but would tend to become itself a new subject in the development of Giacometti's art. Indeed paralyzed between the immense number of details and the impossibility of managing the totality of the head, Giacometti now found a device from which he derived an axis hitherto unknown in the history of sculpture. Placing the model farther away in his field of vision, Giacometti created two coordinated effects: first, by increasing the distance he blurred the details; but consequently with the strict observation of the model in his field of vision, in his perception that distance considerably reduced the figure. "In order to see the whole, the model must be put farther and farther back. The farther away it is, the smaller the head becomes," Giacometti was to say. By wanting to see reality frontally and re-create it as he saw it, to the extent that he could only see it at a distance while respecting the representation of that distance embodied in his subject, Giacometti not only satisfied his earliest obsession in the presence of reality; but at the same time that he laid the foundation for a new standard of perception, he articulated new ways of seeing and of representation. In other words, Giacometti found his style. In the more and more reduced and threadlike figures of this period, which today appear to us the moment of genesis of Giacometti's own style, at first we see only the organic product of the sculptor's method and the mark of his scrupulous respect for what he saw in the essential modality of the act of looking, based on the irreducible axis of the distance between the observer and the object observed. This experience and discovery of integrating distance into the act of re-creating a model was undoubtedly experienced by Giacometti as a new challenge to adhere to the reality of his subject; and in numerous attempts he would lament the drastic reduction of his sculpture to such a small scale. However, his singular genius lay in knowing how to transform that experience of the impossibility of direct adherence to the model into a powerful and convincing metaphor of human existence, governed

14-115. LITTLE MONSTERS
1953 - Bronzes, each 10.5 × 3.9 × 2.6 cm
Private collection

116. FIGURINE
ca. 1959 - Bronze, height 10.8 cm
Private collection

117. FIGURINE
ca. 1959 - Bronze, height 7 cm
Private collection

118. HEAD OF A MAN
1959 - Bronze, height 6 cm
Private collection

by the relations of distances and by an immediacy delayed by the remoteness of frontality itself.

In liberating the academic rules from the "real dimension"—one that is only the representation of things as we know them and not as we see them—Giacometti validated the phenomenological proposition conceptualized in the realm of perception by the philosopher Maurice Merleau-Ponty.

From this point of view, it is the totality of the dimension of the artistic act that has been modified by Giacometti's experiments. We could not know how to find the conclusive reality or truth of the model in itself because the distance between the model and the work of art is in itself the fulcrum for modification of perception. The artistic act, as Giacometti conceived it, is the product of a continuity between the artist's vision and the model, and the work of art undertakes to re-create this revelation of the artist's vision and his seeing it. Therefore, the act of looking, as much as the subject observed, is the basis for the truth of representing the model; that is why the representation of the distance occurs in the artistic act, as a necessary and positive value in re-creating what one sees.

It is true that the reduction and elongation of the statuettes produced at this time led Giacometti to

his style, but it is obvious that what we identify as its value is not the arbitrary result of anecdotal distortion. On the contrary, until 1947, his style progressively revealed the artist's clear intention of showing us, in works that are nothing more than outlines, the act of his looking at his model.

At the beginning of the war, Giacometti stayed in Paris, where he was friendly first with Balthus, Tal Coat, and Derain, and later with Sartre and Simone de Beauvoir, and continued to meet frequently with Picasso, his longtime friend and admirer. Giacometti then moved to a hotel room in Geneva, where he lived from 1942 to 1944. It was at that time that he met Annette Arm, who was to become his wife.

After the Liberation of Paris in 1945, Giacometti returned there and went back to the studio in the rue Hippolyte-Maindron, which Diego had been able to maintain exactly as Alberto had left it. We now turn a new page and find Giacometti standing before the work of his mature years.

1. Pierre Schneider, *Les Dialogues du Louvre* (Paris: Denoël, 1972).

119. THREE PERSONAGES
     1949 - Oil on canvas
     Mr. and Mrs. Adrien Maeght collection

# V – Giacometti: The Painter

It is the figure of Giacometti the sculptor who is remembered and esteemed, in contrast to Picasso, whose sculpted work and its importance are recent discoveries. Giacometti's large, elongated figures allow rapid identification, overshadowing his pictorial work, which is on the same place as his sculpture and is a kind of extension of it, and which some may even prefer. From his earliest years, Giacometti pursued the threefold artistic path of painting, sculpture, and drawing, without establishing any hierarchy of importance.

His experimental years, in contrast, were devoted exclusively to sculpture, but obviously the end of his sculptural experiments offered the painter and draftsman an opportunity to develop.

Therefore, in contrast to the sculptural work of his mature years, which was the product of the slow development of his artistic thought, his painting was born in 1937, providing we exclude the works of his youth. Imbued with Giacometti's vision, the pictorial work continued, reflecting the relative permanence of his essential ideas.

From the portrait *The Artist's Mother* (ill. 107) or *Apple on the Sideboard* (ill. 110) from 1937, to the superb *Portrait of Maurice Lefebvre-Foinet* (ill. 169), done in 1964, and all the subjects that Giacometti took on, while noting the often great differences in stages of completion, all are nevertheless of the same stylistic mold, and the same artistic vision prevails in all these works.

If Giacometti's pictorial work must hold our attention and merit consideration independently of the sculpture, since it is equally successful, it is because the painter, perhaps rather more than the sculptor, stated fully and determinedly in his work the ambivalence of his position. Located between his concern, which some might call academic, for a faithful representation of his subject or model and his acute knowledge of those principles that have stood for modernity ever since Baudelaire, his position was not only ambivalent, but also paradoxical. Looking back, it is even possible to think that the sculptor's work constitutes a privileged means of access. Painting, more than drawing, permits the visibility of successive layers in the formation of the figure, and it is for this reason that it teaches us about Giacometti's general method, and leads us to glimpse the understanding underlying the artist's interpretation of the art of his time. Perhaps paint does this rather better than sculpture, which is more stiff, massive, and definitive.

Given Giacometti's obsession to produce a head, to realize a landscape, that is, to reconstitute the subject, his pictorial work forcefully demonstrates that the subject takes absolute precedence to the situation, and that the situation extends beyond the topographical space that frames it. The painter also produced a head, using the range of his understanding of modern art.

In each of Giacometti's pictures, everything starts with a sort of enigma about the subject's position because the space it occupies is paradoxical. Until 1957, Giacometti placed the subject, often by a multiplicity of internal frames, or by the multiplication of graphic indices, in a situation or space whose elements denoted spatial coordinates. But these graphic connections, distributed around the figure, are an invisible environment; they do not represent or depict anything, but rather adhere to, or establish, the frontier between the visible and the invisible. Paradoxically, these graphic connections, which streak the context of the figure, also form the threads of a limitless environment. After 1957 Giacometti abandoned this graphic execution of context in favor of a gray or ocher nebulousness, which appears on the virgin ground of the canvas, and out of which the figure appears in its turn. This internal oscillation between the visible and the invisible, proximity and distance, appearance and disappearance, laid the foundation for the success of these works, and it also located the very direction of modern art, thus establishing Giacometti as a master in his own time.

In spite of its apparent diversity and innumerable techniques, modern art displays logic and meaning; for modern art looks at the invisible before it looks at us. From that viewpoint, whatever beguiles the eye, registers useful control, and amplifies our feelings with what is visible and can be appropriated, deploys a superb array of boundaries, delays, obstacles, and oppositions at the limit of what we can visually accommodate. But, on the other hand, we may consider painting a means of gaining access to visual impressions we will never have. Such is the paradox of art that it reckons essential what we do not see; and that what we do see is only the singular predisposition, aspiring each time to that primeval and final threshold of inspiration, of vision before and after our paltry gaze.

In Western civilization, in the area with which we are concerned, awareness of the invisible culminates in two successive stages. The passion for the

120. THE ARTIST'S MOTHER
1949 - Oil on canvas, 38 × 27 cm
Mr. and Mrs. Adrien Maeght collection

divine precedes the fascination with the limitless. Beyond this are superficialities, applied arts, retinal fantasies, phantoms: the cancerlike empire of talent, in which the representation of those traits displaying mastery of the visible multiplies itself anarchically.

Haunted by the boundless, that is, by the progressive unconcern that is its impulse, in the visible modern art rearranges the various procedures and techniques of signification, or, more precisely, of inference. Therefore, what concerns us in the visible must above all be extreme doubt regarding the stability of the visible, insinuating and suggesting in the very form of the sculpture the space of the immaterial whole. The compact and formless veins of ore that we call the pedestal in Giacometti's sculptures are only unrecognizable locations, from which he eradicates himself and from which the statues' verticality extends; in this shapeless mass

dwells the real object, the first and last form, elusive and ungraspable, of the representation.

Although we can discern *Three Plaster Heads* (1947) (ill. 122) or the face in *Portrait of Annette* (1951) (ill. 125), we do so through a deception in the representation; on all sides these figures are eaten up by their context, which coils around and absorbs them. We assist in this absorption, in which it is hard to differentiate between the figure's being discernible and its disappearance into Giacometti's technique, which reflected a growing unconcern with differentiation. When in 1958 Giacometti painted the *Tall Standing Nude* (ill. 158), in which he reconciled the gap between the discernible and the invisible by the merest suggestion of the figure's outline, he produced a masterpiece of his vision. The finality of this picture lies in its representing passage of time by a space that cannot be reduced to the conjectural contingencies of form. Certainly this form, this play of signs, this figurative shorthand, together make up the unique source of our assimilation of the representation, but the residual value of the form here is no more than transitory, indicating a direction toward what is beyond the form.

To experience something by means of its representation is first of all to be confronted by the synergy of a play of forms and colors available to the shadowiness of the re-creation of something that already shares our recognition, agreement, consent, and culture.

Unfortunately, Giacometti's work encounters strong resistance from some of our contemporaries, or elicits their eminent scorn for his portrayal of a painter facing his model, which they pronounce too classical or academic. Although for many decades Giacometti confined himself to working in a classical frame of mind, this does not at all invalidate the innovativeness of his vision. It is not innovation for its own sake that is relevant, for that is only the product of a withdrawal, an inconsistency, an essence, a feeling about things hereafter acquired through and in visibility. The enigma and innovation in Giacometti's work, on the threshold of the visible world, present us with new paths that lead us to the edge of what does not emerge from the outline or vibrate in the color, but for which the outline and the color betray an irresistible attraction: that which endlessly appears and disappears. Put succinctly, Giacometti paints what he does not recognize. Such was the character of the artist who dominated his period. Giacometti left what he knew to work with what he did not, but his work

121. THE ARTIST'S MOTHER
1951 - Oil on canvas, 92 × 72 cm
Musée national d'Art moderne, Centre Georges Pompidou

122. THREE PLASTER HEADS
1947 - Oil on canvas, 73 × 59.5 cm
Alberto Giacometti Foundation, Zurich

123. STUDIO WITH "MAN POINTING" AND THREE APPLES
    1950 - Oil on canvas, 56 × 41 cm
    Private collection, Beverly Hills

124. PORTRAIT OF ANNETTE
1950 - Oil on canvas, 72.5 × 34.5 cm
Emanuel Hoffman collection Kunstmuseum, Basel

represents an exhaustive approach to this enigma, without the hope of ever weakening its power.

In this regard, Giacometti's entire body of work is his masterpiece, and the producer of this work was that unnameable authority that commanded him "to make only by unmaking." Two of his famous models, James Lord (ills. 138–140) and Yanaihara (ills. 209–211), have recounted their experiences sitting for their portraits: the acute anxiety that gripped the painter facing his canvas; the rapid execution, their faces rendered in a few brush-strokes; then sitting after sitting; the exhausting work of correction, of obliteration, of layering, of superimposition; until finally the sitter saw in one wonderful look, achieved he knew not how, what had previously been unseen. True art, far from being agreeable to the eye and the dedication of talent, is another burden to the spirit, a laceration, a trial. The chief mission of art is to remove us from the human realm to the very limit of vision, of the senses; when "the eye hears," said Claudel, that is, when it loses its power of recognition and contends with blindness. Art is always beyond art. In the last six years of his life, when Giacometti painted a portrait—portraits were by then his main interest—he concentrated his whole attention on re-creating what he saw, precisely because he wanted to master what is beyond art. It was not enough for him to master the features of a face, or even the character of his sitter. He wanted to paint the impossible: that point where two glances meet. That limitless, unique moment when we meet another seemed the most extreme point of reality to Giacometti—that which constitutes reality, such as it is. But, conversely, if he could paint a look, he would know how to make a face: "Because what most interests me now is to produce the curve of the eye. That seems to me the most difficult thing. If I have the curve of the eye, I would have the socket as well. If I have the socket, I would have the beginning of the nose, its point, its nostrils, and the mouth. Then everything else would come, even the look, without having to concentrate on the eye itself."

It is not surprising that these are not pictures, but rather continual attempts to catch the look of his models and to re-create its immediate boundary. The idea of completion is irrelevant both to his painting and to his sculpture. Giacometti didn't intend to make art; nor did he wish to master the space of a picture. "I hate having to cover a canvas. Besides, it is always impossible to really finish, whatever it is," he confided to James Lord. Consequently, it seems that Giacometti's pictures only represent earlier levels of their definitive realization,

86

125. PORTRAIT OF ANNETTE
1951 - Oil on canvas, 81 × 65 cm
Alberto Giacometti Foundation, Zurich

126. PORTRAIT OF ANNETTE
1951 - Pencil drawing
Private collection

or, amounting to the same thing, the total of correc-
tions, additions, erasures that allows us to glimpse a
preceding state, one of a multitude to which the
work we are looking at leads. This perception is all
the more poignant because Giacometti's pictures
are more drawn than painted; the formation of the
figures is always no more than the product of a
more or less compact skein of lines. Furthermore, in
these works color plays a secondary role. Giacometti
limited himself to tints, not colors, which permitted
him great variety in tonalities of similar values;
above all, ocher and gray. The black and white lines
serve only to indicate the fleeting passage of his
subject's outline. Giacometti painted the image's
twilight, the threshold of the discernible, but if we
briefly consider the different themes that he used, it
becomes clear that two chief areas of technique
govern their execution.

127. PORTRAIT OF ANNETTE
    1961 - Oil on canvas, 146 × 97 cm
    Kunsthalle, Hamburg

128. LANDSCAPE OF MALOJA
1930 - Pen drawing, 21.5 × 26.5 cm
Alberto Giacometti Foundation, Zurich128.

### Landscapes

The landscapes (ills. 129–131), dominated by views of the neighborhood of the studio on rue Hippolyte-Maindron and panoramas of Stampa, are treated in a uniform manner over their entire surface. This effect of congestion and flatness is due to the fibrous linear networks that saturate the different objects in the picture, and by overlapping, condense them into one organic sequence. It is true that the large masses are discernible, but always on the verge of vanishing, of being diluted in the graphic medium—acute, nervous, continual, and interrupted—which unites the details in a vision both frontal and peripheral, keeping the viewer before the vision, but outside, resisting assimilation.

129. LANDSCAPE OF MALOJA
    1953 - Oil on canvas, 46 × 55 cm
    Private collection, Zurich

130. THE STREET
1952 - Oil on canvas, 73 × 54 cm
Beyeler collection, Basel

131. THE GARDEN AT STAMPA
1954 - Oil on canvas, 89 × 62 cm
Mr. and Mrs. Adrien Maeght collection

132. PORTRAIT OF DIEGO
1951 - Oil on canvas, 80.5 × 65 cm
Kunsthaus, Zurich

133. PORTRAIT OF DIEGO
1959 - Oil on canvas, 61 × 49 cm
Tate Gallery, London

## Portraits

The portraits represent a different expression of his vision, and Jacques Dupin is right to insist on their being called "focus" compositions. He adds: "The line is not so much a definition of forms as it is a challenge to them to appear, revealing themselves in the curve. Their frequency and emphasis are heightened as they near the focus."

In the diachronic display of these portraits, we can watch the progression of that radical emphasis on the face alone, in defiance of its outlines. The nudes and portraits of the fifties, despite the license given to the central subject, are for the most part still arranged in a particular space, with a glimpse of the studio furnishings in the background, or the junction of its walls. In the sixties, Giacometti concentrated exclusively on traces of the likeness. He assembled the features and brought together the essential facial expressions. The shoulders are sketched in; the torso disappears; the vague background is often reduced to a tinted monochrome surface; or, as in some portraits of Caroline (ills. 163–166), a few right angles are hastily drawn like a blind man grabbing a support. Thus the portraits—though we may generalize and include all the pictures—rather than remaining portraits, become more and more suggestions. Giacometti painted suggestions because he sought to convey a convincing likeness, to master reality, to draw out the truth in what he saw; in doing this he also saw the distance, of which he despaired and which precluded his belief that he could really re-create the absolute reality that he saw. Therefore, he painted pointers, signposts, hints, and suggestions, which, when multiplied, cluster around his subject, which emerges from this nest of possibilities.

What establishes Giacometti as one of the greatest contemporary artists is his austere and anguished quest, sometimes successful, sometimes not, for what we will never see, of which he gives us only its shape.

**134. DIEGO READING IN THE STUDIO**
1952–53 - Oil on canvas, 92 × 71 cm
Kunstmuseum, Winterthur

135. DIEGO
1950 - Pencil drawing, 49.9 × 32 cm
Burckhardt-Koechlin Collection
Kupferstichkabinett, Kunstmuseum, Basel

136. BUST OF DIEGO
ca. 1955 - Bronze, 56.5 × 21.5 × 15 cm

## Portraits of Diego

How does one paint emptiness? It seems that no one tried it before Giacometti. For five hundred years paintings were full to bursting, the world pushing in on itself. In his canvases Giacometti begins by expelling the world: his brother Diego, quite alone, lost in a hangar—that's enough. Still we must distinguish the person from his surroundings. Ordinarily, that would be done by emphasizing the outline; but a line is produced by the intersection of two surfaces, and emptiness cannot be a surface, still less can it be volume. One can at least separate the context from the contents by a line, but emptiness is not context. Can we say that Diego is separated from the partition behind him? Indeed not, the background connection exists only when surfaces are relatively flat; unless Diego leans up against it, that partition cannot be a background for him.

Have you noticed the superabundance of white strokes that streak the faces and torsos? This Diego is not tightly sewn: he is only basted, as a seamstress would say. Or might it be that Giacometti wishes "to write luminously on a black ground"? Almost. It's no longer a matter of separating the full from the empty, but of painting fullness itself. It is both single and diverse; how does one differentiate without dividing? The black strokes are dangerous; they might scratch or cause cracks. If they are used to outline an eye or a mouth, we will be led to believe that there are hollows of emptiness on the breast of reality. These white strokes are there to suggest without showing; they guide the eye, imposing their movements on it and then melting from view.

Jean-Paul Sartre
"Les Peintures de Giacometti"
*Derrière le miroir* 65 (1954)

96

137. DIEGO IN THE PLAID SHIRT
   1957 - Oil on canvas, 81 × 65 cm
   Mr. and Mrs. Adrien Maeght collection

## James Lord

Whoever knew Giacometti even slightly certainly heard him say that he was on the point of accomplishing something for the first time in his life. And undoubtedly that was what he thought at the time. But a detached observer would have felt that the particular work that elicited this reaction was not fundamentally different from its predecessors. Furthermore, in all likelihood, it would not appear fundamentally different from those that would follow, some of which would elicit the same reaction. It was far more the expression of his whole creative attitude than simply a statement regarding any work in progress at a given moment. Giacometti might deny it, but I think this is true. In fact, it would probably be necessary for him to deny it because in the burning sincerity of this particular reaction resides the decisive strength of all the others, past and future. If he couldn't prove that something really existed for the first time, it would never exist at all for him. From that almost childlike and obsessive reaction to nature and visible reality comes that authentic originality of his vision.

James Lord
*Un Portrait par Giacometti*
(Paris: Editions Mazarine, 1981)

138. PORTRAIT OF JAMES LORD
1954 - Pencil drawing, 49.8 × 32.5 cm
Private collection

139. PORTRAIT OF JAMES LORD
1960 - Pencil drawing, 46 × 32 cm
Private collection

140. PORTRAIT OF JAMES LORD
1964 - Oil on canvas
Private collection

141. PORTRAIT OF PETER WATSON
1954 - Oil on canvas, 73 × 60 cm
Alberto Giacometti Foundation, Zurich

142. PORTRAIT OF DAVID G. THOMPSON
1957 - Oil on canvas, 100 × 73 cm
Alberto Giacometti Foundation, Zurich

143. PORTRAIT OF JEAN GENET
1955 - Oil on canvas, 73 × 60 cm
Musée national d'Art moderne, Centre Georges Pompidou

144. PORTRAIT OF ARAGON
1946 - Pencil drawing, 52.5 × 37 cm
Private collection

145. PORTRAIT OF GEORGES BATAILLE
1947 - Pencil drawing, 17 × 13 cm
Pierre Matisse collection, New York

### Jean Genet

His statues seem to belong to a bygone age, to have been discovered after night and time—who fashioned them cleverly—had corroded them to give them this feeling, at once soft and hard, *of eternity passing*. Or perhaps, they emerged from a crucible, the residue of terrible heat: the flames extinguished, that is what remains.

But what flames!

Giacometti once told me that he had the idea of sculpting a statue and then burying it. (One immediately thinks: "Let the earth be gentle to it.") Not for it to be discovered, or only much later when he himself and even the memory of his name would have disappeared.

Was this burial an offering to the dead? . . .

His drawings. He only draws with a pen or hard pencil, and the paper is often torn or full of holes. The curves are hard, without gentleness or softness. I think for him a line is a man—he treats it as one equal would another. The broken lines are sharp and give his drawing a sparkling appearance—thanks to the granatic, but paradoxically cloying, material of the pencil. Diamonds. Still more like diamonds because of his way of using white.

Jean Genet
*L'Atelier d'Alberto Giacometti*
(Paris: Marc Barbezat, 1958)

102

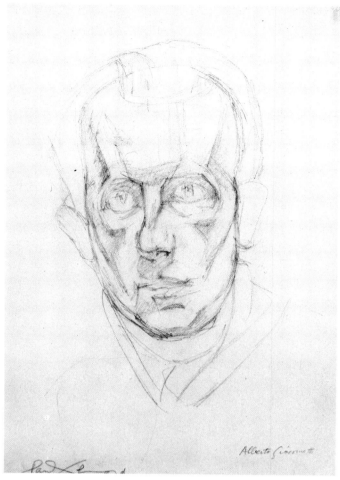

146. PORTRAIT OF PAUL ELUARD
1937 - Pencil drawing, 34 × 32.2 cm
Private Collection

147. PORTRAIT OF JEAN-PAUL SARTRE
1946 - Pencil drawing, 30 × 22.5 cm
Private collection

## Jean-Paul Sartre

One day when he began to draw me, Giacometti expressed astonishment: "What density, what strong lines!" I was even more astonished than he because I thought I had a sort of flabby face, like most people. But he saw each line as a centripetal force. The face came back on itself, like a loop. Turn around: you won't find an outline, nothing but the middle. The line is the beginning of negation, the journey from being to nonbeing. But Giacometti believed that the real is pure positiveness: *there is* being, and then suddenly it is no longer there. But from being to annihilation is not conceivable. Notice how the many strokes he draws are *inside* the form he depicts; see how they represent the intimate relation of the being with himself, the fold of a jacket, the wrinkle on a face, the projection of a muscle, the direction of a movement. All these lines are centripetal: they seek to contract and compress, they force the eye to follow them, and they lead always to the center of the figure. It is as though the face shrinks, the effect of some astringent substance: in a few minutes it will be only as big as a fist, like a shrunken head of the Jivaro Indians.

Jean-Paul Sartre
"Les Peintures de Giacometti"
*Derrière le miroir* 65 (1954)

148. THE TABLE
   1950 - Oil on canvas, 33.5 × 46 cm
   Emanuel Hoffman Collection
   Kunstmuseum, Basel

149. STILL LIFE WITH BOTTLES
1956 - Oil on canvas, 64 × 50 cm
Galerie Beyeler, Basel

150. THE STUDIO
1961 - Oil on canvas, 36.5 × 29 cm
Private collection

151. THE STUDIO
1947 - Pencil drawing, 53 × 35 cm
Private collection

### The Studios

Like the French capital, for which Giacometti titled the portfolio of lithographs *Paris without End* (ill. 250–253) that he executed just before his death, the studio also constituted a subject without end for him as a painter and draftsman.

The artist often recalled the difficulty of his very radical approach, which was to elicit a previously undisclosed emotion from a familiar object. Giacometti's endless series of studios are an exhaustive investigation of ideas of situation, site, and boundaries. Indeed, the studio motif is inherently suited to the painter's vision and technique, which indicate, by a gradual process, the appearance of an outline.

The studio is not in itself a form, but rather a juxtaposition of different viewpoints and, therefore, of various defined boundaries. In the same way, the painter's art proceeding from a juxtaposition of degrees of elaboration of the representation, and the themes of the studio and location could only be the best motifs in this exhaustive, continually renewed search for the undiscoverable boundary.

152. THE STUDIO
   1955 - Oil on canvas, 74 × 50 cm
   Private collection

153. PORTRAIT OF ANNETTE
Pencil drawing, 35 × 32.5 cm
Mr. and Mrs. Adrien Maeght collection

## Annette

After his stay in Geneva between 1942 and 1944, where he met the woman who was to become his wife, Annette Arm, Giacometti never stopped trying to bring out through all possible means and through many portraits the identity of his companion, even up to the last months of his life.

All frontal views, but extraordinarily diverse, this gallery of portraits offers us a rare chance to see the changes and evolution in the artist's style, due to the continual availability of the model.

154. PORTRAIT OF ANNETTE IN A RED BODICE
1961 - Oil on canvas, 55 × 46 cm
Private collection, Winnetka

155. PORTRAIT OF ANNETTE IN A YELLOW BLOUSE
1964 - Oil on canvas, 50 × 40 cm
Alberto Giacometti Foundation, Zurich

156. PORTRAIT OF ANNETTE
   1964 - Oil on canvas, 70 × 50 cm
   Alberto Giacometti Foundation, Zurich

157. STANDING NUDE WOMAN
1959–60 - Bronze, height 278 cm
Musée national d'Art moderne, Centre Georges Pompidou

## The Nudes

Can the nude be considered an important subject in Giacometti's work? Certainly the painter, the sculptor, and the draftsman, by turns, practiced the art of capturing the appearance of the female nude. But if we look even briefly at the catalogue of his work, it is obvious that in distorting and reaching beyond the anatomical identification of his subject, the artist was not aiming at a re-creation of the body. Faithful to his vision, it was rather the impalpable outline, the immaterial density of distance and otherness which were his real subjects. Apart from the nude, that is, its anatomical identity, Giacometti had a single desire: to delineate the location revealed by the presence of the silhouette.

158. TALL STANDING NUDE
    1958 - Oil on canvas, 155 × 69 cm
    Galerie Beyeler, Basel

**159. ANNETTE**
1951 - Pencil drawing, 50 × 32 cm
Private collection

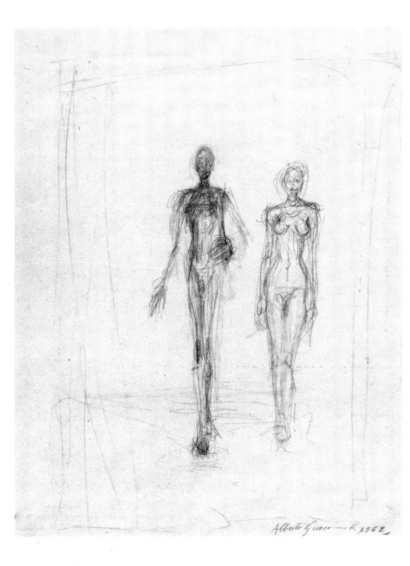

**160. COUPLE**
1962 - Pencil drawing, 63 × 47 cm
Private collection

161. SMALL NUDE
  1964 - Oil on canvas, 60 × 49.5 cm
  Alberto Giacometti Foundation, Zurich

162. PORTRAIT OF MARGUERITE MAEGHT
1961 - Oil on canvas, 145 × 95 cm
Mr. and Mrs. Adrien Maeght collection

163. PORTRAIT OF CAROLINE
1962 - Oil on canvas, 100 × 81 cm
Kunstmuseum, Basel

164. PORTRAIT OF CAROLINE
    1962 - Oil on canvas
    Musée national d'Art moderne, Centre Georges Pompidou

165. PORTRAIT OF CAROLINE
    1965 - Oil on canvas, 127 × 80 cm
    Tate Gallery, London

## A Portrait by Giacometti

The following day was my ninth as a model. I was beginning to be able to discern what Giacometti was doing as he worked, to notice the way in which he used his various brushes, as well as the colors he used and when he used them. Although he always had a bouquet of eight or nine brushes in his hand, he never used more than three—two narrow ones with long, tapering ends made of sable, and another larger one, shorter, thicker, and harder. One of the two thin brushes dipped in black was used to form the head, gradually building it up with numerous tiny superimposed strokes. After having worked thus

for some time, Giacometti would soak the brush in his dish of turpentine and press the point between his fingers. Then, still with the same brush, he would start to work in white or gray. From that I deduced that he would begin to draw the outline and develop the volume of the head at the same time as he put in the highlights. A little later he would take the other brush and begin to work over what he had already painted, using only white. When that occurred, I knew that the head would soon enter the phase of "disintegration." Then, after a certain time, the thick brush would come into

118

166. PORTRAIT OF CAROLINE
1965 - Oil on canvas, 130 × 80 cm
Tate Gallery, London

167. PORTRAIT OF NELDA
1964 - Oil on canvas, 54.5 × 46 cm
Alberto Giacometti Foundation, Zurich

play, handled more freely and impetuously than the thin ones. It was used to define the space behind and around the head, to indicate the outline of the shoulders and arms, and finally to complete the "disintegration" process by effacing the details. Then, with the first thin brush, Alberto would start all over again with the black, endeavoring to draw from the void, so to speak, a semblance of what he saw in front of him. And so on, untiringly.

The model is very important. Both Yanaihara and Caroline also had the feeling that to pose was to take an active part in the work. It wasn't easy, I

know. On the contrary, Genet considered posing completely passive. He stopped posing because he had the impression that he was becoming an object. That seems to me a very literary attitude.

James Lord
*Un Portrait par Giacometti*
(Paris: Editions Mazarine, 1981)

119

168. PORTRAIT OF AN OLD WOMAN
1965 - Oil on canvas, 88 × 65 cm
Private collection

169. PORTRAIT OF MAURICE LEFEBVRE-FOINET
1964 - Oil on canvas, 65 × 45.5 cm
Alberto Giacometti Foundation, Zurich

170. HEAD OF A MAN I (DIEGO)
1964 - Oil on canvas, 45.5 × 35 cm
Alberto Giacometti Foundation, Zurich

171. HEAD OF A MAN II (DIEGO)
1964 - Oil on canvas, 45.5 × 37.5 cm
Alberto Giacometti Foundation, Zurich

## Male Busts

Surprising as it may seem, after a review of Giacometti's work—most especially the pictures—the subjects are no longer discernible. For this painter who was so obsessed by the manifestation of his subject's presence, the space depicted is not so much a designated setting as it is anguished space, streaked, full of overpainting, stratified by the impossibility of making the subject that obsessed him appear.

Whatever the subject, a head, a corner of the studio, or a street, it was only a vehicle, a transitory resolution, a stage in precession, a block in a labyrinth, which affirmed the genetic development of the picture. In this sense the true subject of Giacometti's pictures was painting itself—in the visibility of its progress—beyond his ability and expertise to represent the seen object, which remains a deception and an enigma.

Giacometti's modernity, if we want to use this term, lies in this indifference to his subject, in the transformation of its representation into a purely pictorial undertaking.

That the painter was keen to begin again and again, without tiring, portraits of Annette, Caroline, and Diego is conceivable—and in the end admirable—only because of his clear awareness of the unfolding of an idea that goes beyond the picture's circumstances and themes.

172. HEAD OF A MAN III (DIEGO)
     1964 - Oil on canvas, 65 × 45.5 cm
     Alberto Giacometti Foundation, Zurich
173. HEAD OF A MAN IV (DIEGO)
     1964 - Oil on canvas, 50 × 40.5 cm
     Alberto Giacometti Foundation, Zurich

## My Reality

Since I first drew or painted, I always have done painting and sculpture to catch hold of reality, to defend myself, to nourish myself, to grow; to grow in order to defend myself better, in order to attack and grab things; to go as far as possible in all directions; to protect myself against hunger, cold, death; to be as free as possible to seek—with the most appropriate means for me today—to see better, to understand better what is happening around me; to be as free and as substantial as possible; to expend, to exert myself as much as possible in whatever I do; to pursue my experience, to discover new worlds; to fight my battles—for pleasure? out of joy?—for the pleasure of winning and losing.

Alberto Giacometti

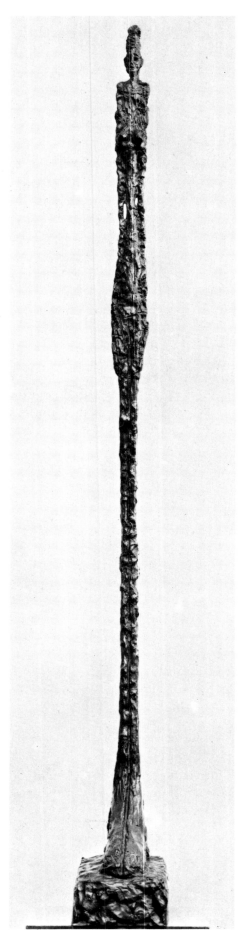

174. WALKING MAN
1947 - Bronze 171 × 23.5 × 32 cm
Alberto Giacometti Foundation, Zurich

175. TALL FIGURE
1947 - Bronze, 202 × 22 × 41.5 cm
Alberto Giacometti Foundation, Zurich

176. STANDING WOMAN
1948 - Bronze, 167.5 × 16 × 34 cm
Alberto Giacometti Foundation, Zurich

# VI - Sculpture (1946-1966)

"The explanation came to me soon after a day when I was carrying a piece of sculpture to an exhibition. I picked it up with one hand and put it into a taxi. I noticed it was light, and I am always irritated by those huge sculptures that five strong men couldn't lift. I am irritated because the man in the street weighs nothing; in any case he is much less heavy than the same man dead or unconscious. He balances on his legs. You don't feel his weight. That is what I unconsciously wanted to show in refining my silhouettes, that lightness."

Having worked face to face with a model, the procedure was familiar to him; and having ascertained the impossibility of re-creating what he saw, Giacometti tried working from memory. Thus, by taking into consideration the distance he had just experienced and discovered, he would be able to establish a new axis of observation. He would know exactly how to arrange the material yielded up by his memory, to place it at the ideal distance, which would allow him to grasp its outline without being rendered powerless by the innumerable details of the face.

After 1940, but more obviously after 1945, Giacometti's concerns had undergone a change, although he himself did not yet know it. It was no longer the re-creation of the physical likeness that interested him, but the re-creation of the model's identity beyond the physical reality of the face, that is, the sum total of those characteristics that mark the humanity and absolute uniqueness of each person.

We should not, therefore, be surprised that from this moment Giacometti's art underwent a reduction, a subtraction, an obliteration of the physical material, resulting in a synthetic approach to the positioning of the figure in distance and space. Consequently, a vision of distance and the verge of disappearance would henceforth torment the artist confronted by the continual labor of subtracting material in order to render the indefinite outline of the blurred model's silhouette.

The importance, volume, and density of the bases of Giacometti's sculpture between 1932 and 1966, sometimes metaphorically substituted by the image of a chariot, cage, table, closed passage, box, are easily explained. That dematerialization that Giacometti imposed on his subject, even sometimes virtually eliminating the figure, obliged him to reinforce proportionally the base of this vague, unreal figure; the base then becomes concrete reality, the physical and identifiable support of the manifestation of the subject's identity.

## Woman on a Chariot

*Woman on a Chariot* (ill. 177), executed between 1942 and 1943, is midway between post-Surrealist stylistic concerns and the artist's definitive style; it signifies new ideas in Giacometti's work. Although this statue may be the result of a desire to impose a religious or cult image of divinity, the characteristic slimming of the following years is discernible, and the heavy base incorporates the artist's old concern with real movement. The theme of *Woman on a Chariot* was to be taken up again in 1946, and then again in 1950 in a work titled *The Chariot* (ill. 187). In 1947 Giacometti decided against any more miniaturization in his statues and, in fact, from this date, began a very fruitful period, as much in the realm of sculpture as in drawing and painting.

177. WOMAN ON A CHARIOT
1942–43 - Bronze, height 157 cm
Private collection

## The Hand - Man Pointing

This group of sculptures is a bridge between the old ideas, which still predominated in some subjects, and the already clear vision of the future work.

Undoubtedly, as we have just seen, the master sculptor—although he would reject such a word—found the right form through which to express an essentially emotional content. For all that, in three works of this period Giacometti had not yet completely given up the Surrealist themes that dominated his work in the preceding epoch.

*The Hand* (ill. 179), *Man Pointing* (ill. 180), and *The Nose* (ill. 185) are still dominated by a certain taste for provocation, for a mysterious setting, for introducing the unseen or the distorted, all of which exemplify Surrealist imagery.

179. THE HAND
1947 - Plaster, 65.5 × 79 × 3 cm
Alberto Giacometti Foundation, Zurich

178. HEAD ON A ROD
1947 - Painted plaster, 50 × 12.5 × 19 cm
Alberto Giacometti Foundation, Zurich

## Head on a Rod

By contrast, *Head on a Rod* (ill. 178) represents the endurance of the theme of death among the artist's obsessions, a staggering portrait of the head of a corpse, related to the tragic episode of his youth in 1921 when, in the bedroom of an inn, he witnessed the horrifying death of a friend, the old librarian van M., whom he had met in southern Italy. The remoteness of the memory made it possible for Giacometti to synthesize the vision and to dispel the painful reminiscence of his past in a powerful evocation of a head like a petrified mask.

## Walking Man - Tall Figure

*Walking Man* (ill. 174) and *Tall Figure* (ill. 175) show at once the great dichotomy in the artist's representation of the sexes. "I always depict a woman as immobile and a man as walking," Giacometti was to say. This dichotomy underlines the ever-present influence of Egyptian art, in which the difference between the sexes is denoted by the position of their feet.

In *The Nose* (ill. 185)—which reverts to the same viewpoint as *Point to the Eye* (ill. 77)—and in these two statues, we see the establishment of the absolute authority of the frontal vision. Also found in his painting and drawing, this is not at all accidental, but is organic to Giacometti's vision.

180. MAN POINTING
1947 - Bronze, 176 × 90 × 62 cm
Tate Gallery, London

126

181. THE CITY SQUARE
1950 - Painted bronze, 21 × 63.5 × 44 cm
Emanuel Hoffman Collection
Kunstmuseum, Basel

182. MAN WALKING IN THE RAIN
1948 - Bronze, 45 × 77 × 15 cm
Alberto Giacometti Foundation, Zurich

183. THREE MEN WALKING
   1948 - Bronze, 72 × 40 × 40 cm
   Maeght Foundation, Saint-Paul-de-Vence

184. THE FOREST
1950 - Bronze, 58 × 64.5 × 60 cm
Maeght Foundation, Saint-Paul-de-Vence

In his process of dematerializing and unmaking the figure, Giacometti arrived at the idea that the corollary of elongating the vertical axis would be to reduce the lateral thickness of his statues. Thus what remains materially is the minimum necessary for the delineation of the figure, which takes on meaning only from a distance, where all that matters is the appearance of the form and its inevitable remoteness. In this way Giacometti understood how to create the exact equivalent of his vision of reality itself, fleeting, distracted, fugitive, unapproachable. He had, thereby, mastered a paradox: his statues appeared deprived of all weight and proportion and to have become ghosts.

In 1948 Giacometti was much preoccupied with the idea of a composition involving several persons, and in this mode he produced *Three Men Walking* (ill. 183) and *The City Square* (ill. 181). These sculptures began a cycle of which *The Forest* (ill. 184) and *The Glade* (ill. 188), both done in 1950, would be the most accomplished. This cycle of works, more than any other, has often been interpreted in moral terms. In these groups of people, separate, and often going in different directions, Giacometti expressed human solitude, the loneliness of each person in a group; and it seems likely

that these moral and existential concerns had long been part of the artist's humanist preoccupations. But perhaps it isn't this particular aspect that gives these works their importance: it should not be forgotten that while Giacometti was involved at this time with Sartre and his circle, he always reacted strongly to any attempt to impose a literary or psychological vision on his work, stating that his only subject and problem was perception itself.

These sculptures with multiple figures can be divided into two groups: in one, all figures are frontally aligned, such as in *Four Figurines on a Base* (ill. 193) or *Four Figures on a Pedestal* (ill. 190), from 1950; in the other, figures are in different positions, placed on a flat base. The two are very different in feeling.

After having successfully created single figures in 1947, Giacometti, temporarily satisfied, pursued a new track, seeking to place several figures on one surface. *Three Men Walking* is about different kinds of directionality, a problem tackled again in *The City Square*, with the additional ideas of intermediate spaces between people, the representation of interpolated emptiness, and internal distance.

## The Forest - The Glade - The City Square

In this series, of which *The Forest* (ill. 184) and *The Glade* (ill. 188) are the masterpieces, we begin to understand better the uncompromising will of the sculptor to create, based on his observation of reality, a parallel artistic reality whose intensity is analogous to what he sees.

It was no longer enough for Giacometti to re-create the frontal distance that he felt existed between the model and himself. He thought of his art as a totality both surrounding and existing between the subjects making up his creation, as the record of his own feelings when confronted by reality. The sculpture is an autonomous reality made up of the sum of the distances between the figures, and the personal experience of the artist is thus incorporated into an independent microcosm. But for Giacometti, *The Glade* and *The Forest* also represent a return of the impression of his first childhood feelings about the natural surroundings of Stampa, and he described the forest thus: "For many years of my childhood, in one corner of the forest, the straight, bare trunks (without branches almost to their tops), through which blocks of gneiss could be seen, always seemed to me like people who had stopped in midstride to speak to each other." In the same way, *The Glade* found its origin in the sculptor's own experience. He related the incident: "The sensations I experienced the preceding autumn at the

185. THE NOSE
    1947 - Painted plaster, 82 × 42 × 40.5 cm
    Kunstmuseum, Basel

186. FIGURINE BETWEEN TWO BOXES WHICH ARE HOUSES
1950 - Painted bronze, 30 × 54 × 9.5 cm
Alberto Giacometti Foundation, Zurich

sight of a glade (really more of a wild meadow with trees and shrubs at the edge of the forest) attracted me very much. I would have liked to paint it, to make something of it, and I left it with much regret."

These are important indications; they signal that the creative process always derives from a personal, emotional, and perceptual base, and that Giacometti, like all great artists, sought in his work to create his own former experiences. The countryside of Stampa, with its gnarled trees, its rocky crevasses, and its mountain peaks, can be found in Giacometti's approach to his material, in the striations and abrupt movements, scratches and elongations, in the firm bases. The compositional problems of internal distance in *The Glade* or *The Forest* are doubled in the latter work, as well as in a different version of *The City Square* (*Composition with Three Figures and a Head*) (ill. 189), from 1950, by the introduction of a bust, or a head, on a pedestal. By using these contrasting elements, Giacometti introduces a gradation and a disproportion, which adds an expressive and monumental dimension. In addi-

tion, the presence of these heads, and of their gazes confronted by the viewer's, places the visual field where the doubled distance of the figures is interspersed, the figures appearing in the distance and in the intersection of gazes. The frontal figures on the base, or pedestal, have a slightly different feeling.

## The Chariot

In that same year of 1950, a very fertile one for the artist, came *The Chariot* (ill. 187), the last sculpture of that theme. However, in this last work it is no longer movement for its own sake that interests Giacometti; in fact, the wheels are fixed on their base. Rather the artist has created a final synthetic figure from observations made in 1938 when he was hospitalized for several months after having been knocked down by a car: the model was the cart that the attendants used to carry their equipment. *The Chariot* is clearly the definitive form, carried out in Alberto's personal style, of this theme, a sacred image of great elegance again confirming the enduring Egyptian influence on his inspiration.

187. THE CHARIOT
1950 - Bronze, 167 × 62 × 70 cm
Alberto Giacometti Foundation, Zurich

188. THE GLADE (COMPOSITION WITH NINE FIGURES)
1950 - Bronze, 59.9 × 65.5 × 52 cm
Alberto Giacometti Foundation, Zurich

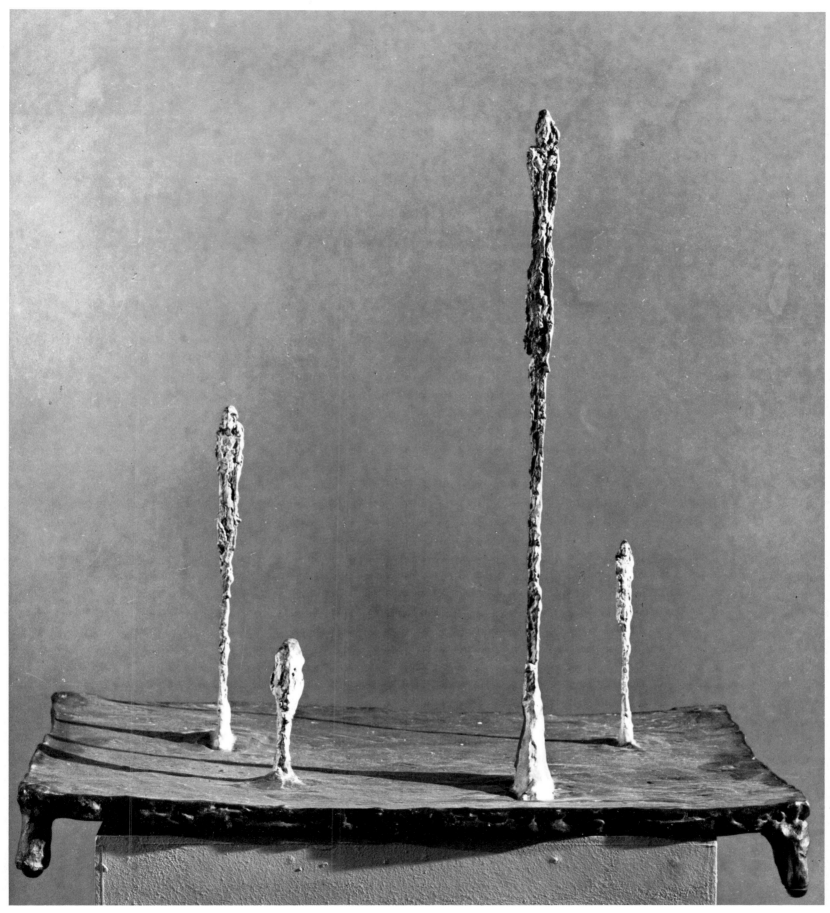

189. THE CITY SQUARE (COMPOSITION WITH THREE
FIGURES AND A HEAD)
1950 - Painted bronze, 56 × 56 × 42 cm
Alberto Giacometti Foundation, Zurich

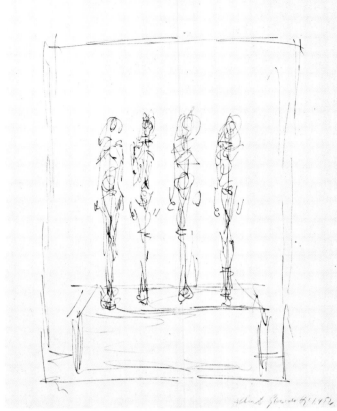

191. FOUR FIGURINES ON A PEDESTAL
1950 - Pen drawing, 31.5 × 23.5 cm
Private collection

190. FOUR FIGURINES ON A PEDESTAL
1950 - Painted bronze, 76 × 41 × 17 cm
Alberto Giacometti Foundation, Zurich

## Figurines on a Pedestal - Caged Figures

For *Four Figurines on a Base* (ill. 193), Giacometti drew on his observation of a show danced by
prostitutes, and it was obviously the elusive and
evanescent character of these women that struck
him. In setting his figures on pedestals, his intention
was to elevate them and to impose their fascinating
domination on the viewer; but from this very fact
the pedestals become sanctuaries or ramparts pro-
tecting the inaccessibility of the figures. Their remoteness is all the more peremptory in that the
pedestals' solidity, like a piece of furniture beneath
the figurines, contrasts with the slenderness and
fragility of these figures, of whom only their silhouettes are seen.

*Enclosed Figures* and *The Cage* (ill. 194), from
1950, recapitulate in the same way his experience
and vision.

192. FOUR FIGURINES ON A PEDESTAL
   ca. 1950 - Painted plaster, height 20 cm
   Mr. and Mrs. Adrien Maeght collection

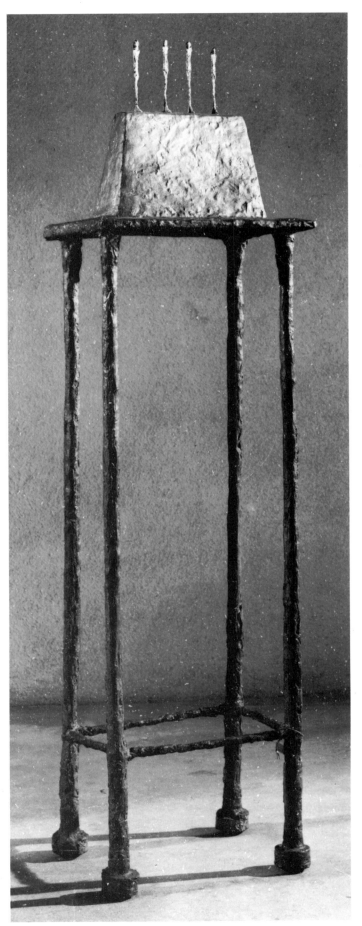

193. FOUR FIGURINES ON A BASE
1950 - Painted bronze, 162 × 42 × 32 cm
Alberto Giacometti Foundation, Zurich

194. THE CAGE (WOMAN AND HEAD)
1950 - Painted bronze, 177 × 39.5 × 38 cm
Alberto Giacometti Foundation, Zurich

195–198. MAN CROSSING A SQUARE
1949 - Bronze, 68 × 80 × 52 cm
Alberto Giacometti Foundation, Zurich

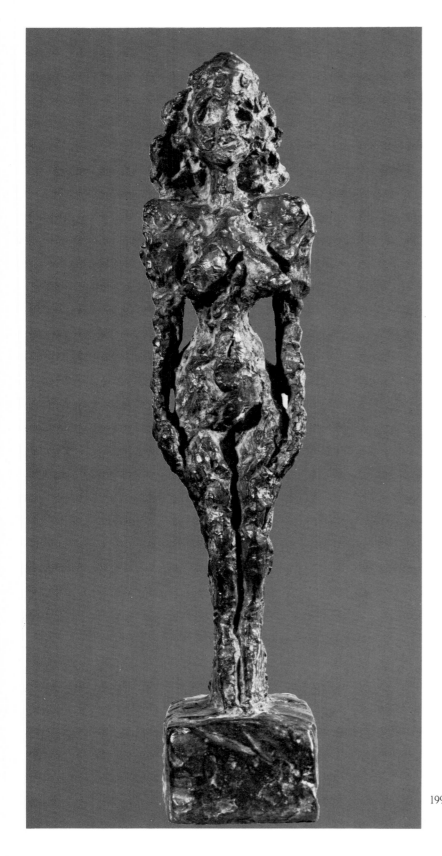

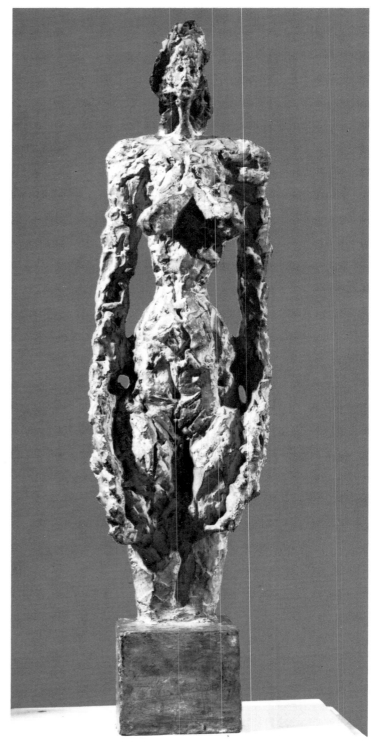

200. NUDE (FIGURINE ON A CUBE)
1953 - Painted bronze, 57.5 × 15 × 15 cm
Alberto Giacometti Foundation, Zurich

199. STANDING NUDE III
1953 - Bronze, 54.5 × 12 × 16.5 cm
Alberto Giacometti Foundation, Zurich

201. NUDE WOMAN
Painted bronze, height 25 cm
Mr. and Mrs. Adrien Maeght collection

202. THE CAT
1951 - Bronze, 29 × 80.5 × 13.5 cm
Alberto Giacometti Foundation, Zurich

203. THE LEG
1958 - Bronze, 220 × 30 × 46.5 cm
Alberto Giacometti Foundation, Zurich

## The Dog - The Cat - The Leg

From the onset of the period when the artist again exhibited his work in New York and Paris, he became even more famous and numerous exhibitions succeeded one another, with his first retrospective in Basel in 1950. In this same year he was invited to represent France at the Venice Biennale, but he withdrew his work in a show of support for his friend Laurens, whom he thought had been badly treated. He was invited again to the biennale in 1956, and in 1962 he received the international accolade of the Grand Prix. Retrospectives of his work were held as often in Europe as in America, as were one-person exhibitions in galleries; in addition he participated in group shows. Rich and famous, his work exhibited in the world's greatest museums, Giacometti remained the same: a native of the mountains of Stampa to which he returned each year, back to his mother who would model for him. He stayed in the same wretched studio, tenacious in his pursuit of his work, doubting continually in order to better understand it, yet keeping his door open to all who wished to enter. Alberto Giacometti was an unusual man; everyone who knew him agreed that his was a demanding artistic ethic, and affirmed his profound humanity, his taste for discovery, his scorn for convention, his disdain for the

204. THE DOG
1951 - Bronze, 45 × 98 × 15 cm
Alberto Giacometti Foundation, Zurich

position that his fame could have given him, and his single-minded approach to the work yet to be done. His answer to the question as to whether he would save a Rembrandt painting or a cat from a burning house, explains him better than any analysis—he would save the cat. This man, who sat each day face to face with another to try to catch the truth of his model, made a remark one day, which is revealing of his sincerity: "I would give all my work for one conversation." He devoted the last sixteen years of his life not so much to cataloguing new experiences as to deepening his fundamental vision of reality, of art, and of the reality of art. The problem of style, which had formerly been for many years the major subject of his experiments, was henceforth emphatically affirmed by the fertile matrix of his vision. In the whole stylistic statement of his work, he could now freely conduct his experiments to capture a likeness, an identity. Although he sometimes allowed himself to be seduced by his desire for symbolic expression, as in *The Dog* (1951) (ill. 204), which he identified as a self-portrait, or *Man Turning Upside Down* (1950), or indeed, even *The Leg* (1958) (ill. 203), the rest of his work now developed with classical concision and austerity.

205. SEATED WOMAN
1956 - Bronze, height 77 cm
Musée national d'Art moderne, Centre Georges Pompidou

## The Women of Venice

Two main themes would dominate his last years, two themes constantly reworked. In his work, Giacometti admitted success only in terms of future potential, never in terms of current accomplishment. The motionless female nudes and busts of men (and occasionally busts of women), usually from models, are the two essential threads of his creative work.

The series of motionless female nudes is dominated by two large groups that sum up the artist's work. Created in 1956 for the Venice Biennale, the series Women of Venice (ills. 206, 207) offers a magnificent range of variations of the artist's perception of his model. The second series on the same theme is Tall Figures (ill. 208), executed in 1960. The Women of Venice form a coherent group, with a naturalistic approach and minimal configuration, a visible inventory of the inner stages of Giacometti's definitive style. Absolute vertical divisions of space, totems and divinities, the figures in this group are the artist's crowning achievements. These elongated, threadlike figures, poised on the point where appearance meets disappearance, or advancement meets recession, because of their lack of thickness, represent in their very variety the symphonic end of Alberto Giacometti's quest. Two complementary observations may be made about this lauded masterpiece. When we reflect that Giacometti followed the teachings of Antoine Bourdelle, and that, therefore, Rodin's work at that time must have been central to the young artist's ideas on the meaning of sculpture, we are struck by the fact that Giacometti simply inverted the methods of his elders, although that has never been acknowledged.

Rodin's chief merit lies in his having freed sculpture from the conventions of statuary. Concerned with his model and the laws of anatomy, Rodin changed the reproduction of his subject in the organic expansion of its appearance, which gave meaning to the formal, peripheral autonomy of the figure and offered him great power of expression. This growing proliferation of details, or parts of the figure, leads the viewer's gaze over the totality of the unfolding volume in space. Before a Rodin sculpture, the viewer's glance is caught, entwined in the twists and turns of a sort of emphatic narration of anatomy. Consequently, without injuring the whole, each part of a figure is invested with the

206. WOMAN OF VENICE VIII
1956 - Bronze, 122 × 14 × 35.5 cm
Alberto Giacometti Foundation, Zurich

207. WOMAN OF VENICE VI
1956 - Bronze, height 133.5 cm
Maeght Foundation, Saint-Paul-de-Vence

expressive display of its form, with a fascinating and meaningful autonomy.

The great sculptures that Giacometti executed at the end of his life, from the series Women of Venice to Tall Figures, or even to the sculpture *Walking Man* (1960), invert the vision of the old master. In opposition to his expression of forms and thick curves of contour, Giacometti puts his catabolic vision of an immaterial vertical line; in contrast with Rodin's bending, turning figures, he presents his unique frontal vision; rather than the expressivity and particularity of his details, Alberto offers a synthesized single conception; and finally in opposition to the sensuality of depictions of Balzac, Giacometti presents nudes totally devoid of any sexual representation.

That brings us to the significant second observation about these two large groups of figures: in these nudes, anatomy is obliterated; the sexual representation of woman is erased. In this sense, Giacometti did not abandon the vision that ruled over the development of the series Unpleasant Objects (ill. 75) in the Surrealist period: he had not yet renounced his fascination with horror and sexual murder. Instead, he transferred the symbolism of *Woman with Her Throat Cut* (ill. 80) and the violence of *The Couple* in a symbolic manifestation that suppresses the woman's basic identity—her femininity. This diagrammatic presentation of a woman transformed into a petrified goddess undoubtedly expresses an unconscious wish to negate the sexual differences. This denial, this symbolic castration, already present in *Walking Woman* (1933) (ill. 100), is also compensated for by a characteristic spreading at the base of these sculptures. Francis Ponge was right to observe: "Take away the big feet and leaden boots of Alberto Giacometti's figurines, and there is nothing left." In fact, what hangs by no more than a thread has in its base an imposing origin. It is as if in order to raise and refine itself further, the statue breathed into its base that material density shed while emerging. The same observation may be made of several Busts of Diego (ills. 214–218) and one of Yanaihara (ill. 212), which enthrone a shrunken head, unfleshed, disproportionate, on strong shoulders and a thick chest.

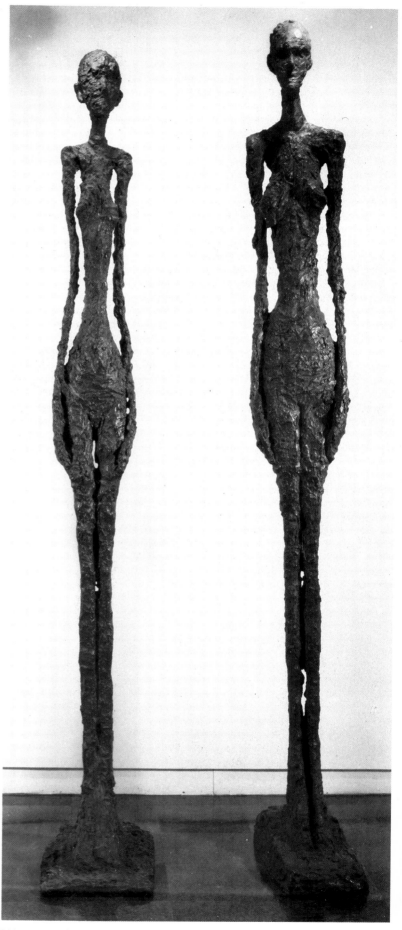

208. TALL FIGURES I AND III
1960 - Bronzes, heights 260 and 278 cm, respectively
Private collection, United States

145

209. PORTRAIT OF ISAKU YANAIHARA
1957 - Oil on canvas, 81 × 65.5 cm
Alberto Giacometti Foundation, Zurich

210. PORTRAIT OF ISAKU YANAIHARA
1960 - Oil on canvas, 55 × 46 cm
Private collection

## Portraits of Yanaihara

Between 1956 and 1961, Giacometti worked with Professor Yanaihara (ills. 209–213). This was a period of great crisis for the artist, and from then on we notice several modifications in the last busts. In his work on Alberto Giacometti, Jean Genet relates this distressing episode: "All the time that he struggled with the face of Yanaihara (one can imagine the face offering and then denying itself, as its likeness passed over the canvas, as if trying to protect its unique identity), I saw the moving spectacle of a man who never deceived himself, but was always lost. He buried himself ever deeper in inaccessible regions with no exit. But he managed to come back up. His work is both gloomy and dazzling." Sartre also observed: "At that time he was truly desperate."

The conditions of this crisis are identical with those preceding. Perhaps it was the strangeness of the oriental face that began it; Giacometti felt once more the immensity of the contradiction between style and likeness, which he had tried to overcome

in the past. By the artifice of moving the model farther away in space, he seemed to have resolved the first contradiction between the unity of the face, the unity of the subject, and the dissemination of detail. Moreover, it was from this observation that he appeared to have succeeded in at last resolving with one stroke, the contradiction between art and reality. The artist's style appeared improved by his having overcome these contradictions.

Face to face with Yanaihara, Giacometti felt once more the illusory character of this device. The style, the organic solution, had become a technique of appropriation that no longer left him any doubt about the impossibility of representing the absolute reality of his model's face. The putting together of the original strokes that would define the style of the figures appeared to Giacometti as simply a technique, and the true artistic value of the style inserted itself between the artist and reality, deterring him from ever grasping the truth of the thing observed. Consequently, the artist could not hope

146

211. PORTRAIT OF ISAKU YANAIHARA
1960 - Oil on canvas, 84 × 72 cm
Private collection, Paris

212. BUST OF ISAKU YANAIHARA
1962 - Bronze, height 35 cm
Private collection

in any way to establish a resemblance between his model and the re-creation he wanted to make. Confronted with Yanaihara, Alberto despaired, and would continue to despair until his death, this arising from his understanding of the character of his style, which he now saw as only the impossibility to which this conventional configuration had led him. Jean Genet observed: "Not only do his statues come upon us from very far away, from a remote horizon, but wherever you are in regard to them, they make it seem that you who are looking at them, are below.

They are on a remote horizon, elevated, and you are at the bottom of the hill. They come hurrying to meet you and to pass beyond you."

It was exactly this flight into the distance, this passing by the viewer, which dissolved all his hope for a resemblance. When faced by Yanaihara, Giacometti wanted to sculpt the analogous presence of Yanaihara, to master the absolute likeness of the face and its gaze; but he was attempting the impossible, his undertaking doomed to defeat, and he knew it.

148

213. PORTRAIT OF ISAKU YANAIHARA
1956 - Oil on canvas, 81.5 × 65.9 cm
Musée national d'Art moderne, Centre Georges Pompidou

214. BUST OF DIEGO
1954 - Painted plaster, height 35 cm
Mr. and Mrs. Adrien Maeght collection

216. HEAD OF A MAN ON A ROD
1956–58 - Plaster, 42 × 10 × 15.5 cm
Alberto Giacometti Foundation, Zurich

215. BUST OF DIEGO
1954 - Bronze, height 39 cm
Musée national d'Art moderne, Centre Georges Pompidou

## Busts of Diego

Throughout his last years, after the painful experience of his portraits of Yanaihara, Giacometti concentrated on creating busts, above all, on two important groups: those of Annette; and a masculine series for which Chiavenna, Diego, and Lotar posed.

## The Painted Sculptures

At various times, and well before that decisive crisis with his Japanese model, Giacometti had plumbed the ambiguity of the dematerialization that his representations of people had undergone. To embellish this excessive reduction, Giacometti found a corrective: to paint his statues. Not only the plaster works, but also the bronzes sometimes underwent that treatment. According to one anecdote, he first painted one of his works to give it a new density, while preparing for an opening. In an interview with David Sylvester, the sculptor stated that "a sculpture seems dull when it isn't painted; painted, it looks almost as one sees it." Later he said:

150

217. BUST OF DIEGO
1955 - Bronze, 56.5 × 21.5 × 15 cm
Alberto Giacometti Foundation, Zurich

218. NARROW BUST
1954 - Bronze, height 41 cm
Mr. and Mrs. Adrien Maeght collection

"In 1951, I painted a whole series of sculptures. But in painting them, one could see what was missing in the form . . . it made the deficiency of the form stand out. Then I could no longer delude myself that I had created something by painting if there was nothing underneath. Then I would have to give up painting them and try to shape the form. Just as I had to sacrifice the whole person in order to make the head." Aware of the illusory character of using paint on sculpture, confronted by Yanaihara and by successive models until the end, Giacometti began to carry out modifications on the form. From 1961 on, he abandoned his celebrated style: the distribution of mass between the head and the chest now tended toward homogeneity; reduction and dematerialization were eliminated, resulting in a massive materialization, tactile, immediate, and close to his subjects. They are no longer set in an imaginary distance, and because of this fact, the challenge of appearance/disappearance was also disavowed on the axis of distance and flight. Now the heads are faces above an assembled mass that serves both as base and as chest.

219. DIEGO IN A WINDBREAKER
1953 - Bronze, 35.5 × 28 × 10.5 cm
Alberto Giacometti Foundation, Zurich

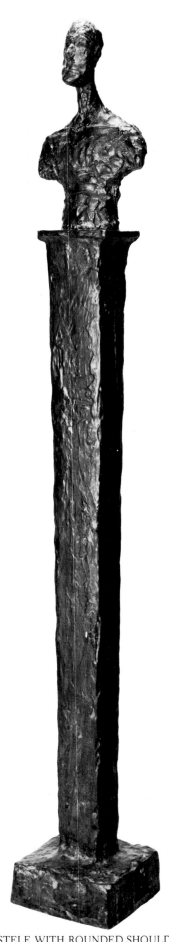

220. DIEGO IN A SWEATER
1954 - Bronze, 49 × 27 × 21 cm
Private collection

221. STELE WITH ROUNDED SHOULDERS (DIEGO)
1958 - Bronze, height 166 cm
Maeght Foundation, Saint-Paul-de-Vence

222. NUDE FROM NATURE (ANNETTE)
1954 - Bronze, 53 × 15 × 20 cm
Mr. and Mrs. Adrien Maeght collection

223. LARGE SEATED WOMAN (ANNETTE)
1958 - Bronze, 83 × 23 × 35 cm
Maeght Foundation, Saint-Paul-de-Vence

## Busts of Annette

The nine busts of Annette (ills. 224, 225) are a collection of idols, whose grace, distinction, and presence are a manifestation of the final homage rendered by the sculptor to one of his favorite models.

Viewed alongside the busts of Annette, which radiate plenitude, the last busts of men done in 1964 and 1965 (ill. 226) are all the more poignant. These somber faces, austere and meditative, inhuman as masks, with their prominent, arched brows shadowing their dreaming gaze, are moving testimony from the artist a few months before his death.

All that remains of one's existence, in one's final concentration, is dedicated to endless contemplation, a gaze without object.

These final masterpieces no longer aspire to produce a likeness of the model. In these works, Giacometti petrified his last thoughts, the stoical loneliness of a condemned man who knows he is going to die; his last effort embodying the appearance of silent thought.

224. ANNETTE VI, II, IV
1962 - Bronzes, height 60 cm
Private collection

225. ANNETTE V
1962 - Bronze, height 47 cm
Private collection

226. BUST OF CHIAVENNA
1964 - Bronze, height 40 cm
Private collection

227. BOUQUET OF FLOWERS
1953 - Oil on canvas, 42 × 33 cm
Mr. and Mrs. Adrien Maeght collection

228. DINING ROOM AT STAMPA
1955 - Pencil drawing, 48 × 46 cm
Private collection

# VII – Giacometti as Draftsman and Lithographer

The often repeated counsel that he had heard from Bourdelle's lips during his apprenticeship at the Academie de la Grande Chaumière, Giacometti himself reiterated in explaining his creative work: that drawing occupies the chief position in a painter's or sculptor's activity.

The celebrated English painter Francis Bacon unhesitatingly formulated this judgment in 1975: "For me Giacometti is not only the greatest draftsman of our time, but among the greatest of all time."

Apart from the sheer quantity of his drawing and its importance in his work, its influence is confirmed by the fact that, as we have seen, his painting is an organic outcome of the primacy of graphic structure.

In Alberto Giacometti's work, the function of drawing is twofold: that of knowledge and of emotional delineation, and according to the subject he was dealing with, one or the other would govern his actions, but without ever eliminating the complementary function. From his earliest years and throughout his life, Giacometti pursued the careful study of those works he admired. In the same way as we never see a work so well as when we describe what we see, so copying, besides supporting the act of seeing, is essentially in accordance with understanding and analyzing what is seen in a work, of which the immediate totality of its cohesion threatens the temporary need to grasp the connecting contours and the internal articulation. Giacometti affirmed that copying in this sense is not necessarily

229. CRUCIFIXION AFTER MATISSE
Pencil drawing, 32 × 25 cm

230. COPY AFTER A SELF-PORTRAIT OF CHARDIN
Pencil drawing, 26 × 16.5 cm

231. FUNERARY FIGURES
Pencil drawing, 17.5 × 11 cm

reproduction, but rather an attempt to reassemble in the matrix of one's own feeling, the goings and comings, the transitions, the seams, the points and lines of a successful whole. Such success by its very nature often makes invisible to the uninformed gaze the laborious work of building up the planes and contours that created it. This investigation of, and encounter with, junctions and intersections and encroachments is the analytical work of the copier. For Giacometti, this work was about knowledge and recording: "For some years I have known that the act of copying is the best means of recording what I see, and in my own work the little I know of the outside world—a head, a cup, or a landscape—comes from copying it. The two activities are complementary." Giacometti wrote this in 1965 when he was desperately trying to abandon any artistic methods that he judged false to his obsession of grasping reality without interposing either will or artistic vision between it and himself. He commented on his recent dislike of copying, the result of his rejection of such methods: "Nowadays I only copy works of art very rarely. The deviation between

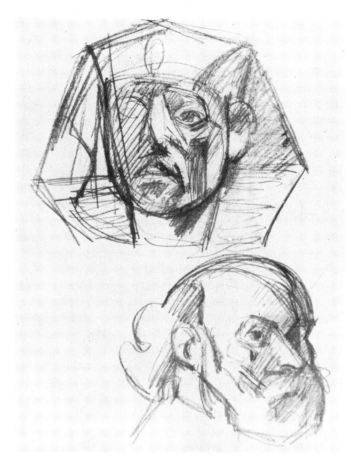

232. COPY AFTER A PORTRAIT OF POPE INNOCENT X
BY VÉLASQUEZ
Pencil drawing, 25 × 20 cm

233. HEAD OF SESASTRIS III
COPY AFTER A SELF-PORTRAIT BY CÉZANNE
Pencil drawing, 31 × 24 cm

any work of art and immediate reality has become too great and, in fact, only reality now interests me, and I know that I could pass the rest of my life copying one chair." Undoubtedly, Giacometti's reasoning was necessary to the final development of his thought, but with regard to the artist's catalogue of copies, it seems to have little foundation.

When he addressed himself to a seminal work of art, Giacometti never treated it as something outside his daily reality. The greatness and importance of these copies should for the most part be considered on the same level as all his drawings: the artist was never separated from his own vision. it is never this or that masterpiece copied by Giacometti that we consider, but the artist's methods and feelings toward a work on a subject that proves to be a configuration rendered by an illustrious predecessor. With regard to these copies, which the artist accumulated throughout his life, often in the margins of books of reproductions, the function of knowledge was tightly bound to the function of emotional delineation, and out of the intimacy of this conjunction grew the work of Alberto Giacometti.

234. STUDY OF TWO MALE HEADS
AFTER A SUMERIAN SCULPTURE
Pen drawing, 27 × 21 cm

235. PORTRAIT OF PIERRE LOEB
1946 - Pencil drawing
Musée national d'Art moderne, Centre Georges Pompidou

236. PORTRAIT OF ELIE LOTAR
1951 - Pencil drawing, 55 × 34 cm
Private collection

Since the observation of reality through drawing thus similarly affected how the artist saw both his daily surroundings and earlier masterpieces, it is also notable that this same activity, this same method of working, appeared in two important media: in what are properly called black-lead drawings and in lithographs. There is no valid reason to introduce any hierarchy between the two, since the process and their effects are similar for the simple reason that Giacometti drew his lithographs on paper kept for that purpose, mechanically transferred to the stone. Herbert Lust's complete catalogue of Giacometti's graphic work records no fewer than 350 works, most lithographs, some engravings. A number were done to accompany the work of the poet André du Bouchet, as well as that of Georges Bataille, Michel Leiris, René Char, and Jean Genet, of whom he often made portraits.

Giacometti's drawings are the umbilical cord of his entire body of work. Perhaps better than any other artist, Giacometti knew how to reveal through his drawings the scope of the question of seeing and of the work of art.

These drawings represent uncertainty and inquiry, a gathering together rather than a dispersion. The inquiry is primarily about the location of his subject. That is, he excavates and draws—especially in still lifes and landscapes—the surroundings, a network, a possibility of place, which by strokes constantly redrawn becomes a probability of manifestation. But the subject's surroundings are also on the edge of vision, the incomplete space of its grasp, and Giacometti reproduces this suspension of seeing by the emergence of the whiteness of the page. Jean Genet was correct in writing: "The strokes are there only to give form and solidity to the whiteness. If you look closely, it is not the stroke that has style, it is the white space contained by it. It is not the stroke that is solid, it is the whiteness."

237. PORTRAIT OF LOUIS CLAYEUX
    1953 - Pencil drawing, 50 × 32 cm
    Private collection, Paris

The guiding inquiry in the hidden struggle, and the conjunction of retraced strokes and whiteness, releases space from the uncertainty of the outline. "In a reflected passion, which dims all the lineaments," wrote André du Bouchet, the subject materializes in the impossibility of fixing its outlines. Giacometti's stroke does not outline or hold; it does not realize the form; it puts together a beginning, suggests a preliminary state of the breaking up of the appearance. The sensitive outline of the subjects, the striated drawing of the planes, the instability of the accumulation of connections lead us to the main point of Giacometti's vision, poised between the act of scrutiny and the feeling of never being able to appropriate what is seen. This twilight understanding of the world is quite other than ascetic. Giacometti built a dwelling for contemplation, and his act is worthy of remaining in man's memory: it is the culmination of Western spirituality. Beyond his artistic success, Giacometti established an exception to the equivalence between vision and ethics.

238. THE ARTIST'S MOTHER
1963 - Pencil drawing, 47 × 31 cm
Private collection

239. THE ARTIST'S MOTHER READING
1963 - Lithograph, 65 × 50 cm
Alberto Giacometti Foundation, Zurich

240. THE ARTIST'S MOTHER BY THE WINDOW AT STAMPA
1963 - Lithograph, 65 × 50 cm
Alberto Giacometti Foundation, Zurich

241. THE ARTIST'S MOTHER
  1958 - Pencil drawing, 50.2 × 32.7 cm
  Private collection

242. INTERIOR AT STAMPA
ca. 1964 - Pencil drawing, 56.5 × 38 cm
Alberto Giacometti Foundation, Zurich

243. THE CHANDELIER AT STAMPA
Pencil drawing, 26 × 45.5 cm
Private collection

244. HOTEL ROOM I
245. HOTEL ROOM II
    1963 - Pencil drawings, 50 × 33 cm
    Alberto Giacometti Foundation, Zurich

248. STANDING MAN AND THE SUN
    1963 - Lithograph
    Alberto Giacometti Foundation, Zurich

246. HOTEL ROOM III
1963 - Pencil drawing, 50 × 33 cm
Alberto Giacometti Foundation, Zurich

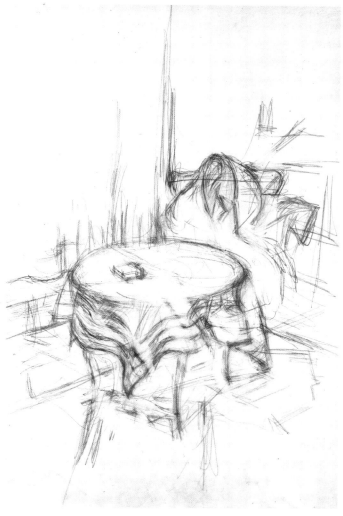

247. HOTEL ROOM IV
1963 - Pencil drawing, 50 × 33 cm
Alberto Giacometti Foundation, Zurich

249. HOTEL ROOM V
1963 - Pencil drawing, 50 × 33 cm
Alberto Giacometti Foundation, Zurich

250–253. PARIS WITHOUT END (ILLUSTRATIONS 10, 12, 14, 69)
Text and illustrations by Alberto Giacometti
Unfinished work of 150 lithographs
Edition of 250 copies, published by Tériade, 1969
Bibliothèque nationale, Paris

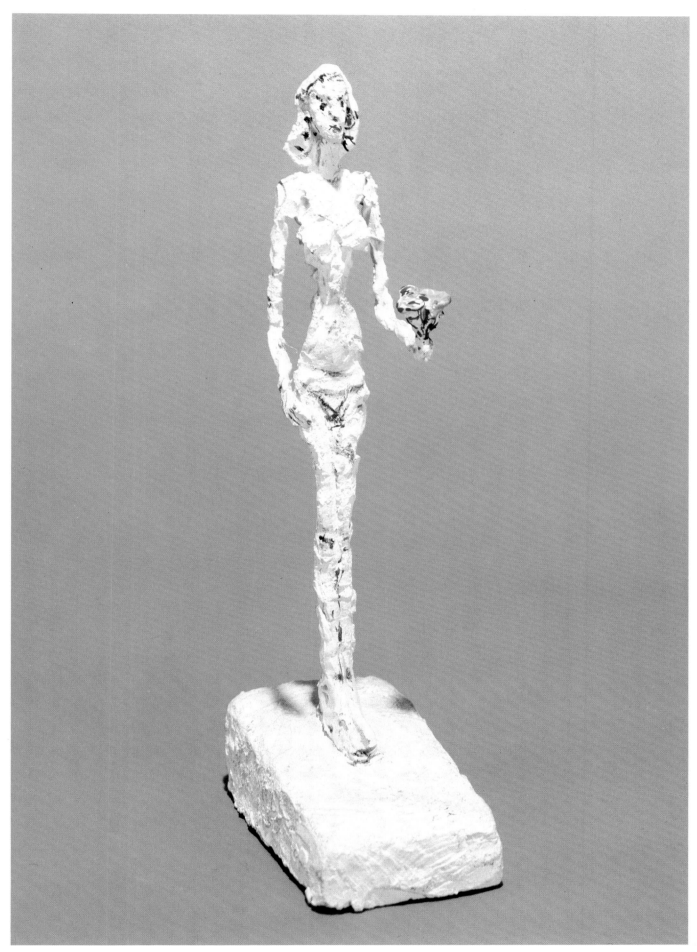

254. WOMAN OFFERING A BOUQUET
1950 - Plaster
Mr. and Mrs. Adrien Maeght collection

255. ALBERTO GIACOMETTI
Photograph by Man Ray

# BIOGRAPHY

1901 *Alberto Giacometti was born 10 October, in Borgonovo, near Stampa, on the Swiss-Italian border, first child of Giovanni Giacometti and Annetta, née Stampa. Two other sons and a daughter would follow. Diego would design furniture and help his brother in the creation of his sculptures. Bruno would become an architect. The family settles in Stampa in 1906 and takes its vacations in Maloja, near Lake Sils. Giovanni Giacometti, a neo-Impressionist painter, teaches his son to draw.*

1915–19 *Alberto studies at Schiers, near Coire, and is a good student. He is interested in history, natural science, and the German romantics, and devotes his leisure time to drawing. His first painting dates from 1913.*

1919 *Unhappy with the teaching at the Ecole des Beaux-Arts in Geneva, he prefers studying sculpture at the Ecole des Arts et Métiers in the same city.*

1920 *Giovanni Giacometti is appointed Swiss representative at the Venice Biennale. Alberto accompanies his father and discovers the art of Tintoretto, Bellini, Giotto, Cimabue, and the mosaics of St. Mark's. In Rome he discovers Borromini and the Vatican collections, and becomes interested in the Italian Futurists.*

1922–26 *He settles in Paris and enters the studio of Antoine Bourdelle, whose teaching he comes to dislike. He fills notebook after notebook with copies of works he admires. In 1925 he shares a studio with Diego at 37, rue Froidevaux. He is friendly with Laurens and Lipchitz; his work is influenced by Cubism and African art. A bust of Diego and Torso are exhibited at the Salon des Tuileries.*

1927–28 *He rents a studio, which he will keep for the rest of his life, at 46, rue Hippolyte-Maindron. He becomes friendly with André Masson, Michel Leiris, Raymond Queneau, Georges Limbour, Jacques Prévert, Georges Bataille. He shows his "flat" sculptures at the Galerie Jeanne Bucher.*

1929 *He contracts for one year with Pierre Loeb. Favorable articles appear by Michel Leiris in* Documents, *and by Christian Zervos in* Cahiers d'art. *He shows two works at the Galerie Bernheim. To make a living he collaborates with Diego in making lamps and chandeliers for Jean-Michel Frank and jewelry for Elsa Schiaparelli.*

1930–32 *He meets the Surrealists—Aragon, Breton, and Dali, all of them fascinated by* The Suspended Ball. *He has his first one-man show at the Galerie Pierre Colle and produces some political drawings for Aragon.*

1933–34 *He takes part in all the Surrealist exhibitions until his exclusion from their circle in 1935 by Breton, who castigates him for returning to sculpting from life (busts of Diego, Rita, Isabel). He has a private show at the Julien Levy Gallery in New York. His father dies.*

1935–41 *He becomes friendly with Balthus, Tal Coat, Gruber, and Derain, then with Sartre and Simone de Beauvoir. He is injured in a car accident in 1938, and his long period of hospitalization leads him to think about movement and equilibrium, and inspires the sculpture* The Chariot (1950). *Returning to work, he sculpts from memory and makes miniaturized sculptures.*

1942–44 *Alberto settles in a hotel in Geneva, where he meets Annette Arm, who will become his wife in 1949. He collaborates with Albert Skira on the review* Labyrinthe.

1945–48 *In Paris again at his studio in the rue Hippolyte-Maindron, he paints from life, and his sculptures become elongated. He paints some of his bronzes. He has a show at the Pierre Matisse Gallery in New York.*

1949–50 *This is a period of concentrated production, during which he creates some of his finest sculptures. He shows at the Pierre Matisse Gallery in New York as he will again in 1955, 1958, 1961, and 1964. He has a retrospective in Basel, and withdraws his works from the Venice Biennale in sympathy with Laurens.*

1951–55 *He begins producing graphic work, lithographs, engravings, and book illustrations for the works of Georges Bataille, René Char, Michel Leiris, André du Bouchet, and Jacques Dupin. He has the first of many exhibitions at Galérie Maeght (the others will be in 1951, 1954, 1957, and 1961), as well as others in New York, Chicago, and Basel. He receives the order of the Médaille à la Gloire d'Henri Matisse. He meets Jean Genet.*

1956–59 *His series* Women of Venice *is displayed at the Venice Biennale. He makes a series of portraits of Diego, Jean Genet, and Yanaihara. He is asked to design a monument for Chase Manhattan Bank in New York. He has a retrospective at the Kunsthaus in Berne.*

1960–63 *He makes a series of portraits of Annette and of Caroline. He receives the Carnegie Prize for Sculpture in Pittsburgh in 1961 and the Grand Prix at the Venice Biennale the following year. He has exhibitions at the Kunsthaus in Zurich, the Galerie Beyeler in Basel, and the Galerie Krugier in Geneva.*

256. ALBERTO GIACOMETTI
Photograph by Brassaï

257. SELF-PORTRAIT
1963 - Pencil drawing, 50.5 × 32.5 cm
Alberto Giacometti Foundation, Zurich

*1965–66 The Maeght Foundation is established in 1964 in Saint-Paul-de-Vence, with many of his works. He receives the Guggenheim International Award in 1964, and that of the Ville de Paris the following year. He has retrospectives at the Tate Gallery in London, at the Museum of Modern Art in New York, and in Copenhagen. He makes many busts of his last model, Elie Lotar. He leaves his series of lithographs* Paris without End

*unfinished. Jacques Dupin and Ernst Scheidegger make a film in his studios in the rue Hippolyte-Maindron and at Stampa. He is hospitalized at Coire in December 1965 with an infarct. He dies 11 January 1966 and is buried at Borgonovo.*

*The Alberto Giacometti Foundation in the Kunsthaus in Zurich opens in that year.*

*Here is the list of sculptures that I promised you, but I can only list them in a certain order, a rather summary one, without which it wouldn't make any sense.*

*I made my first bust from life in 1914 and continued all through my college days. I still have some of these busts, and I always look upon the first with some nostalgia.*

*At the same time, and even many years before, I did a lot of drawing and I painted. Besides drawing from life and from illustrations in books that I was reading, I often copied pictures and sculpture from reproductions. I mention this because I have continued the same activity, with a few brief interruptions, up until now.*

*In 1919 I was for three days at the Ecole des Beaux-Arts in Geneva, and afterwards at the Ecole des Arts et Métiers in the same city studying sculpture, and I did watercolors in the surrounding countryside and by the lake, and I painted at home.*

*In 1920–21 I lived in Italy. First in Venice, where I spent days looking at Tintoretto especially, unwilling to miss a single detail. To my grief, Tintoretto was pushed aside by Giotto of Padua on the day I left Venice, and he in his turn was replaced some months later by Cimabue at Assisi.*

*I stayed nine months in Rome, where I never had enough time to do everything I wanted. I wanted to see everything and at the same time I was painting, figures, landscapes somewhat in the Pointillist style (I was sure that the sky is blue only by convention, but really red), and compositions based on Sophocles and Aeschylus, whom I was reading at that time (The Sacrifice of Iphigenia, the Death of Cassandra, the Sack of Troy, etc.).*

*I had also begun two busts, one small, and for the first time, I was unable to leave it, I lost myself in it, I forgot myself, the head of the model before me became like a cloud, vague and limitless. I ended by destroying both of them at the end of my stay. I spent a lot of time in museums, churches, and ruins. I was particularly attracted by mosaics and the baroque. I can remember each feeling inspired by each thing I saw. I filled up notebooks with copies. (A marvelous sketch by Rubens I remember now, and the mosaic of Saint Cosmos and Saint Damian, and these are followed by a thousand others, but I must get on.)*

*In 1922 my father sent me to Paris to go to the Academie. (In one way I would have preferred to go to Vienna, where life was cheaper. At that time my desire for pleasure was stronger than my interest in the Academie.)*

*From 1922 to at least 1925 I was at the Academie de la Grande-Chaumière, with Bourdelle. In the morning I sculpted and found the same difficulties I had encountered in Rome. In the afternoon I drew.*

*I could no longer bear sculptures without any color, and I often tried to paint them from life. I kept a few for some years, and then I threw them out to make room.*

*It seemed impossible to grasp the whole thing (we were much too close to the model, and if you began with a detail, a fingernail or a nose, there would never be any hope of getting the whole). But if, on the other hand, you started by analyzing a detail, the tip of a nose, for example, you were lost. You could spend your whole life on it and never get anywhere. The shape would come apart; it would be no more than particles drifting on a vast black emptiness, the distance between one side of a nose and the other is limitless as the Sahara, nothing is stable, everything eludes you.*

*Still, since I wanted to re-create at least a little of what I saw, I began as a last resort to work from memory. I tried to save something from that catastrophe. After some attempts involving Cubism, which were inevitable (it would take too long to explain now), I produced things that were for me the nearest I could come to my vision of reality.*

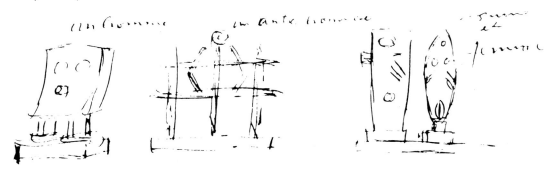

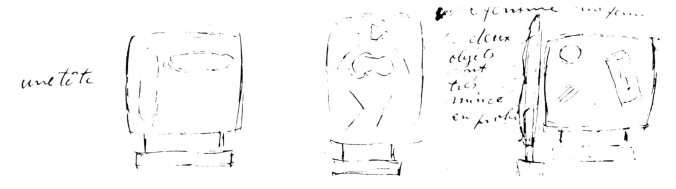

This provided me with a partial vision of reality, but I was still lacking a structure for the whole, an acute aspect that I also saw, a sort of skeleton in space. The figures were never a solid mass for me, they were a transparent construction. After a lot more effort I made cages with a free internal construction, made of wood by a carpenter.

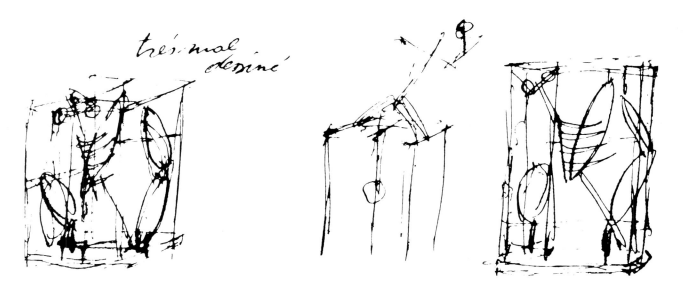

There was a third element that I saw in reality—movement. Despite all my efforts, I found it impossible to sustain a sculpture that gave the illusion of movement, a leg advancing, a raised arm, a head looking sideways. I not only wanted to make this movement real and effective, I also wanted to give the feeling of causing it.

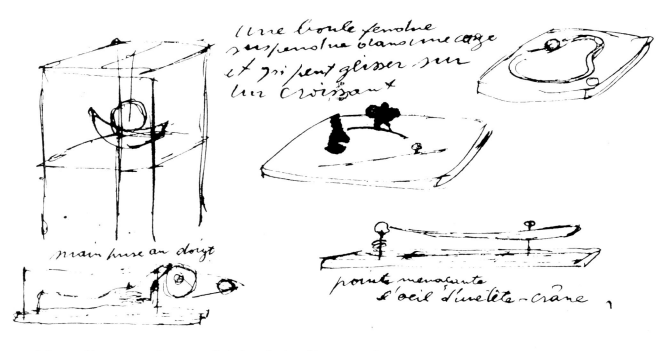

Many objects move because of their relationship to another.

*But all this took me further and further away from reality, and I tended to get enthusiastic only about the construction of things themselves. There seemed to be something too traditional, too precious about these things, and I was disturbed that reality seemed to me quite other. At that time everything seemed a bit ludicrous, meaningless, disposable. I'm saying this in a hasty sort of way.*

*It was no longer the exterior form of people that interested me, but the emotional things in my life. (During all the years before [the time at the Academie], there had always been an unpleasant contrast for me between work and life, one was an impediment to the other, I couldn't find a way out. To copy a body at a certain time—and one that was not important to me—seemed to me completely wrong and stupid, and wasted hours of my life.)*

*It was no longer a question of producing a figure with a superficial likeness, but rather of living without knowing what moved me or what I wanted. But all these things went one way, then the other, inconsistently. I wanted also to find a resolution between placid and solid things and sharp and violent ones. What was produced during those years . . .*

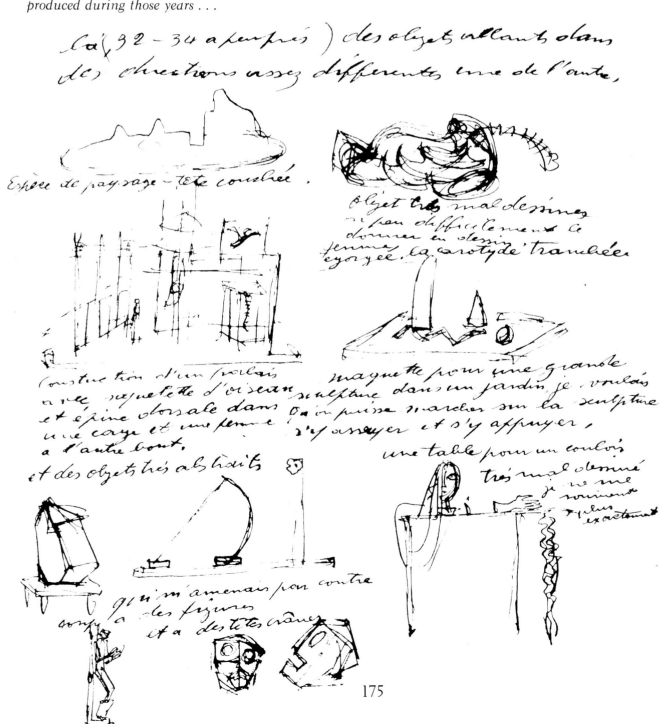

*I saw again bodies that drew me back to reality and abstract forms that seemed true in sculpture, but in a nutshell, I wanted to do the one without losing the other.*

*One last figure, a woman titled $1 + 1 = 3$, whom I've never left.*

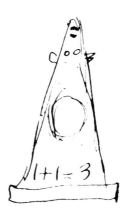

*Then I wanted to make compositions with figures. For that I had to do one or two life studies (quickly), just enough to understand the construction of a head, of the whole figure, and in 1935 I hired a model. These studies took me about a fortnight, I think, and then I resolved to make my compositions.*

*I worked daily with a model from 1935 to 1940. Nothing was as I had thought. A head (I soon stopped doing figures, there was too much of them) became a completely unknown and immeasurable object for me. Twice a year I began two heads, always the same ones, without ever finishing them, and I put aside my studies (I still have the casts).*

*Finally, trying to make something of them, I began to work from memory, primarily in order to know what had stayed with me from all this work (all that time I also drew and painted a bit, almost always from life).*

*But to my horror, when I tried to remember what I had seen, the sculptures became smaller and smaller, they seemed like children, and although I hated these little things and tried again and again I always ended up at the same point.*

*A large figure seemed wrong to me and a little one just as bad; they became so tiny that often with a final cut of the knife, they would disappear into dust. But heads and figures only seemed to have any truth when they were minuscule.*

*All that changed a bit in 1945 with drawing. It led me to want to make larger figures, but to my surprise, they only seemed likenesses if they were long and thin.*

*And that's about where I am today, not where I was yesterday, and I can see straightaway that if I can easily draw old sculptures, I would only have difficulty with those that I made in the last years. Perhaps if I could draw them, it would no longer be necessary to put them in space, but I'm not sure of that.*

*Now I must stop, besides they're closing up, one must obey the rules.*

Letter to Pierre Matisse
1947
Pierre Matisse Gallery, New York

176